MACOUNS

NEW ENGLAND
FARMGIRL

NEW ENGLAND FARMGIRL

recipes & stories *from a* farmer's daughter

written & photographed by

+ JESSICA ROBINSON +

GIBBS SMITH
TO ENRICH AND INSPIRE HUMANKIND

✦ To Grandma Rusin and Grandma Lamothe ✦
Thank you for teaching me the importance
of everything homemade with love.

Jessica Robinson has been an event and floral designer in New England and elsewhere. She divides her time between Canton, Connecticut, and Graham, North Carolina. Catch her blog at newenglandkitchen.com and carolinafarmhousekitchen.com.

19 18 17 16 15   5 4 3 2 1

Text and photographs © 2015 by Jessica Robinson
Front cover photo from Shutterstock.com

Published by
Gibbs Smith
P.O. Box 667
Layton, Utah 84041

1.800.835.4993 orders
www.gibbs-smith.com

Designed by Rita Sowins
Page production by Virginia Brimhall Snow
Printed and bound in Hong Kong

Gibbs Smith books are printed on either recycled, 100% post-consumer waste, FSC-certified papers or on paper produced from sustainable PEFC-certified forest/controlled wood source. Learn more at www.pefc.org.

Library of Congress Cataloging-in-Publication Data

Robinson, Jessica (Event planner)
   New England farmgirl : recipes & stories from a farmer's daughter /
written and photographed by Jessica Robinson. —
First edition.
      pages cm
   Includes index.
   ISBN 978-1-4236-3800-1
1. Cooking, American—New England style. 2. Local foods—New England. 3. Farm produce—New England. 4. New England—Description and travel. I. Title. II. Title:
New England farm girl.
   TX715.2.N48R63 2015
   641.5974—dc23
                                                            2014037245

CONTENTS

ACKNOWLEDGMENTS

This book would not be possible without the love and support of my wonderful husband, Scott. He has always encouraged me to push forward and let no obstacles stand in my way. His belief in my talents and ability has been the driving force behind all my creations. He has always put up with all my crazy, over-the-top ideas and along with the help of his brother, Steve, made them come to fruition. Thank you to Scott's parents, who made me their daughter and supported us both along the way.

Thank you to my grandmothers for teaching me the importance of a solid work ethic, making everything from scratch, and putting love into everything you do.

I am grateful to my family. Growing up on a small farm, we had so many opportunities. We had one of the biggest and most amazing gardens in the neighborhood, where we grew many vegetables and fruits. I was extremely fortunate to have the use of a commercial kitchen in our sugarhouse from a very young age. My mother and father taught me to grow it yourself, make it from scratch, and build it with love and passion using your own two hands. My mother is one of the most talented ladies I know, having mastered the art of baked goods, wedding cakes with handcrafted edible flowers, confections, and canning. My father is a very compassionate and forgiving person, always willing to put down whatever he is working on to help out someone in need.

Thank you to Katie for helping me with photographs, sewing beautiful aprons, and being a great friend. You are one talented lady.

Thank you to everyone who has supported and believed in me along the way. Johanna, I appreciate all your encouragement, long talks, love, and honesty. You are amazing in every way.

FOREWORD
BY TRACEY RYDER

Traveling the back roads of New England with Jessica Robinson while searching out the region's finest orchard fruits and apple cider, maple syrup and handcrafted wines, or artisanal cheeses, yogurts, and baked goods, would be quite an adventure—the kind of culinary road trip, in fact, one wishes would never end. Then imagine the lively conversation that would undoubtedly break out as a group of friends gathers around her farmhouse table, sharing a meal of Hard Cider and Brown Sugar-Marinated Chicken she has prepared and you have another experience you wish could go on forever (complete with Red Velvet Whoopie Pies, please!). These are exactly the kinds of experiences you will enjoy while reading the stories and cooking from the recipes included in *New England Farmgirl: Recipes and Stories from a Farmer's Daughter.*

Jessica is straightforward and completely authentic. She is informed by generations full of rich family history that provide her with solid roots for developing her own new takes on tradition, which she does with warmth and enthusiasm. Each story and recipe is crafted to bring out the best of what New England has to offer: four vibrant seasons, an abundance of exceptional local ingredients, a deep culinary history, and thriving modern-day family farms, all set in a stunningly beautiful regional landscape. From these pages, the fragrance of maple syrup, cider, and cinnamon waft up and capture your imagination.

As someone who has spent the past twelve years completely focused on the local foods movement, specifically with regard to beautifully unique culinary regions and communities, I can tell you that this book is a treasure you will want to refer to again and again. And with Jessica Robinson as your guide, you are in for a meaningful and inspirational journey, whether traveling the region to find the perfect ingredient or while cooking these recipes—all brimming with incredible flavor and character—for your own friends and family. Here's to celebrating the abundance of New England!

—Tracey Ryder, Co-Founder, Edible Communities

INTRODUCTION
THE FARMER'S DAUGHTER

I vividly remember as a young child standing in the garden—clad in navy-and-white Striped overalls, with strawberry blonde hair in pigtails—my toes deeply submerged into the warm soil, helping my parents weed the garden or pick tomatoes. There wasn't a moment where we weren't canning our own tomato sauce or harvesting fresh corn.

My parents were strong advocates of producing as much as they could themselves, and then buying the remainder from other local farms. We raised our own pigs and always cut down a fresh Christmas tree during the holidays. Not only did I learn from these experiences about gardening and growing one's own food, but I also learned the value of family and hard work. Today, my husband and I teach these same values to our own children.

As a kid, I would travel over a one-lane covered bridge and up a narrow pebble dirt road to my grandfather's cottage deep in the woods of Vermont. With no running water or electricity and an outhouse, time stood still there. You could sit on the screened-in porch at night and listen to the peaceful sounds of nature as fireflies danced in the moonlight. I played in babbling brooks and caught black-spotted orange salamanders. It's these fond memories that make my husband and me yearn to travel to New England campsites with our children and rough it, without distractions from the everyday hustle of life. I know that by sharing simple pleasures, my kids will hold those memories deep in their souls and one day share some of these experiences with their own children.

When I was little, my mom baked homemade breads each week to sell to people in our neighborhood, amassing a customer list of about 30 or so. She also created custom cakes and taught me at an early age how to can, cook, and bake a variety of goods from scratch. I helped tap maple trees during sugaring season, hanging galvanized buckets onto trees to collect the maple sap before working long hours boiling the sap into syrup. My parents taught me the art of making pure maple candies, unique confections, and sauces; in their commercial kitchen, I helped develop jam recipes along with cookie mixes to sell.

Naturally and organically produced foods are very important. Simple ingredients, produced without preservatives or chemicals, are ultimately better for you. New England farms and wineries offer a marvelous selection of incredible wines, gourmet foods, and baked goods, as well as fresh produce, local honey, and maple syrup. To me, there is nothing more pleasurable than using such wonderful ingredients, baking from scratch, and watching your guests enjoy not only fresh, natural ingredients but also the love that went into what you created.

There are many ways to bring organic produce into your life. Plant your own garden, or purchase heirloom seeds from Baker Creek Heirloom Seeds or Comstock Ferre & Co., which offer the best in the business. Compost leaves, egg shells, coffee grounds, and ashes from your fireplace to provide rich natural nutrients to add to the soil. The hard work, sweat, and love you pour into the garden will be rewarded with the harvest of quality food.

In this book, you will discover phenomenal places to visit and incredible recipes to enjoy. *New England Farmgirl* also champions the finest tastes of New England, from freshly picked produce to hot-from-the oven breads and excellent wines. The charm and time-honored traditions of New England are deeply rooted in vine-ripened heirloom tomatoes plucked from the field only hours before you bite into them and flavor explodes in your mouth; the quaint old farmhouse overlooking the family-run farm stand; old-fashioned family time; heritage value; and simplified life.

Enjoy this collection of delicious heirloom recipes from a farmer's daughter and her family, along with recipes created right in my own New England kitchen. Thumbing through the pages of this book will be as though you are driving through the rural parts of Connecticut, Maine, Massachusetts, New Hampshire, Rhode Island, and Vermont.

NEW ENGLAND'S BOUNTY

THE BEST OF LOCAL, NATURAL & ORGANIC FOODS

My parents have raised pigs for as long as I can remember. My brother and I were given piglets each spring; we spent time with them, showed them off at fairs, and then in the fall, they would go to the slaughterhouse. We learned from a very young age that death was a part of life. I also participated in 4-H and Future Farmers of America, and in high school, I decided I wanted to keep my pig, Penelope, through the winter and raise a litter of her piglets. At the time, we did not house a barn on our farm. My father said that if our neighbor, who owned an empty dairy barn, was willing to board her, we could keep Penelope. I already had a horse boarding at the same barn, so it was an easy yes. Penelope gave birth to fourteen little piglets that eventually ran loose around the barn.

If you truly intend to eat healthier foods, now is the time to commit to purchasing local produce, dairy, eggs, honey, and freshly baked goods. Consider what you put into your body, and, in the process, help support local farms. If we enrich the core of our bodies with natural foods, our skin, hair, nails, and overall health and well-being will improve.

Buying fresh, local, seasonal ingredients to cook and bake with is a step in the right direction to enjoying a healthy way of living. Look for organic and pesticide-free produce grown in your local area. A large number of local businesses throughout New England are involved in efforts to be more eco-friendly. Without using commercial pesticides, organic farmers go back to natural ways to farm. They utilize crop rotation to confuse pests and renew the soil, adding organic matter into the dirt for natural nutrients. Organic farms plant alfalfa and clover to enrich the soil. When you buy local, you get the freshest ingredients around, while supporting local farmers and the community. Fresh ingredients taste better and are healthier for you, and they make higher quality cakes, pies, and savory dishes. Purchasing locally benefits our environment as well, with less fuel being used to transport products, thus putting fewer emissions into our ecosystem.

All over New England, tasty hand-baked treats and freshly picked crisp lettuce await you at a local farmers market. Displays of homemade jams, breads, and cookies made with all-natural

ingredients and no added preservatives are abundant. Local farmers markets are one of the best places to shop for the freshest eggs, bursting ripe berries, and other wonderful natural foods, all from various farmers. Dozens of pop-up tents line a parking lot or freshly dewed field. Farms each display their daily picked harvest and beautifully packaged canned goods; it's like wandering the freshest grocery store around while soaking in the outdoors.

✦ MARCH FARMS in Bethlehem, Connecticut, is a place we like to visit each fall. Here goats and calves greet you at the fence, and the farm offers the most picturesque views. Ben March is a third-generation farmer who has created an amazing play area for the kids featuring a mini-hayloft, farmhouse, slides, a sand box, and even handcrafted pedal tractors and wagons to ride. Our kids are always completely entertained as they pedal the green tractors around the track, as I'm sure your little ones will be as well. I love that the farm offers an area with picnic tables and umbrellas, as well as hay rides to their field so you can navigate through the corn maze. While at their farm, I enjoy browsing their farm store and picking up cider doughnuts, cookies, and a bushel of apples for freshly baked pies. During the busy fall season, they cannot stock the shelves fast enough with their warm sugar -rolled apple cider donuts. (We always make sure to get at least two packages of them—one for the ride home and one for later!) They also offer local maple syrup and honey, plus fresh apple cider. You can find homemade jams and seasonal produce in their farm store as well.

✦ **LYMAN'S ORCHARD** in Middlefield, Connecticut, dates back to 1741, when it sprawled 36 acres of a very diverse farming operation. They now farm 1,100 acres of farmland, offering a great corn maze for the kids to explore. A few years back, we took our kids to their corn maze and discovered that the design changes each year to be more challenging. John Lyman and his family grow peaches, pears, raspberries, blueberries, and 28 different varieties of apples. As a family, we love to pick our own apples or shop in their Apple Barrel store. Their store also features a spacious deli where you can order a custom-created sandwich, and then munch on it while sitting on their outdoor patio overlooking the picturesque pond with mallard ducks and swans. One of my favorite things about their store is the wide variety of New England–based gourmet foods available. Also, before planning your trip to the orchard, make sure to check their website for the wide variety of events that happen year round. Autumn is a wonderful time to visit the farm to pick your own pumpkins while enjoying the views of fall foliage with ripe shades of green, red, and orange.

✦ **CUPOLA HOLLOW FARMS**, situated in West Suffield, Connecticut, offers a wonderful variety of farm-made jams and jellies, freshly baked cookies, and breads, along with goat milk soap made right on their farm. Suffield, Connecticut, is also a great rural area to take a day trip to, driving around to absorb all it has to offer. Cupola Hollow's goat soaps smell heavenly and are packaged with rustic brown cardboard wrapping paper. Can't get to the farm? You can find owner Cathy and her daughter at many local farmers markets throughout the state and at their own farm stand with wonderful cookies, brownies, and baked goods, along with jams.

✦ **JORDAN'S FARM** is located in Cape Elizabeth, Maine, on 120 acres of rolling hills. The farm overlooks the Spurwink River and is now in its fifth generation of farming. They grow a wide variety of fruits and vegetables, but are best known for their sweet strawberries and corn. The farm stand offers a wonderful selection of Maine products, including locally raised meats, goat cheese, butter, jams, and pickles. This adorable rustic farm stand in a barn-type building is filled both outside and in with seasonal produce grown on this and surrounding farms. Stop here to pick up all of your dinner needs.

✦ **BROOKDALE FRUIT FARM** in Hollis, New Hampshire, boasts beautifully manicured gardens in front of the farm stand. In its seventh generation of family farming since 1847, this farm offers a wide selection of organic produce, grass-fed beef, their own raw honey, and freshly laid eggs. The spacious, earthy farm store, set in a natural barn-style building, features shelves full of locally made maple syrup, jams, jellies, freshly baked pies, and breads. They grow everything from strawberries and salad greens to heirloom tomatoes and pumpkins.

✦ **LARSON'S FARM MARKET** in the picturesque town of Brookfield, Connecticut, has been in existence since 1901 and is in its fourth generation of farming. I adore their open-air farm stand, which boasts vintage wooden crates overflowing with freshly harvested produce, jams, maple syrup and fresh baked goods. They are famous for their sweet corn and the wide selection of farm-grown produce. Fresh, ripe, crisp cucumbers grown on the farm paired with heirloom tomatoes are an appetizing addition to summer dinners. Fall is also a wonderful time to visit their farm, especially during October for their fun and festive haunted corn maze.

✦ **BROWN BOAR FARM**, situated in Vermont, raises heritage pork and beef, along with heirloom vegetables. It is a family-owned farm committed to raising wholesome, all-natural food in an environmentally friendly way. The farm grows heirloom vegetables that return to old roots. They also extend their growing season with greenhouses that are heated by an outdoor furnace, powered with dead timber harvested on their own farm. This helps to eliminate the need for petroleum-based fuels, and the farm is proud of their efforts to be sustainable, with a heritage farming style.

✦ **LAUREL RIDGE FARM**, in Litchfield, Connecticut, raises grass-fed cattle. Their cows graze in fields, and the farm refuses to inject their livestock with hormones or antibiotics. The farm also raises all-natural pastured pork and poultry. The cattle are entirely grass-fed; they receive hay during the winter months with kelp as a mineral supplement. Even better? Grass-fed beef has nearly 75% less fat than grain-fed beef. This family-run farm offers ground beef and steaks packaged in retail packaging, or you can custom order a half or quarter cow. They can also be found at local farmers markets selling their products.

HOW TO FIND LOCAL FARMERS MARKETS IN YOUR AREA

Find a list of farms in your state through the Department of Agriculture. Most states are committed to promoting area farm stands, orchards, wineries, and specialty foods produced in those respective states. You can also find a list of New England area farms on *www.newenglandgrown.com*.

BENEFITS OF BUYING LOCAL, ORGANIC PRODUCE

Be aware of where the products you buy are grown and manufactured. Locally grown vegetables and fruits go straight from the farm to your table. Not only is buying local going to benefit the local farmer, wine producer, and baker, it's also just plain good for you. Natural foods mean no preservatives or additives, limited pesticides, and no artificial ingredients. It also means a healthier appearance, more energy, and, ultimately, a longer life.

Since organic foods are produced without chemical fertilizers, pesticides, or additives, there is a better chance that they are less harmful to the body. And since organic farming means the use of no chemicals, there is also minimal soil, water, and air pollution, offering up a better environment for future generations.

NAVIGATING YOUR WAY THROUGH A CSA SHARE

CSA stands for Community Supported Agriculture. The typical farmers market season runs from early June to mid-October, yet more and more farms offer a CSA program as well. You can purchase a share from your local farm in advance, which helps the farmer with his anticipated costs of the farm operation. In return, you receive shares each week of the farm's bounty throughout the growing season.

PECAN PIE

Here's a recipe from the kitchen of Grandma Lamothe, who has always been very good at creating incredible desserts. With a French-Canadian grandmother, you can rest assured that nothing was ever store-bought.

Serves 6 to 8

PIE CRUST (RECIPE BELOW)

3 LARGE EGGS

1 CUP FIRMLY PACKED BROWN SUGAR

1 CUP LIGHT CORN SYRUP

½ TEASPOON KOSHER SALT

1 TABLESPOON ALL-PURPOSE FLOUR

3 TABLESPOONS UNSALTED BUTTER, MELTED

1 TEASPOON PURE VANILLA EXTRACT

1 CUP PECANS

Preheat the oven to 425 degrees F. Fit a layer of pie crust into a 9-inch pie pan and set aside.

In a large mixing bowl, use a fork to lightly beat the eggs. Add the brown sugar, corn syrup, salt, flour, melted butter, vanilla, and pecans; use a spatula to combine thoroughly. Pour the mixture into the unbaked pie crust. Bake for 10 minutes; reduce the temperature of the oven to 350 degrees F, and continue baking for another 30 minutes. Remove from the oven, allow to cool, and enjoy.

PIE CRUST

(Makes enough dough for a double-crust 8- or 9-inch pie)

2 CUPS ALL-PURPOSE FLOUR

1 TEASPOON KOSHER SALT

⅔ CUP LARD OR VEGETABLE SHORTENING

3 TABLESPOONS UNSALTED BUTTER, VERY COLD

⅓ CUP VERY COLD WATER

In a large ceramic bowl, combine the flour and the salt with a fork. Cut in the shortening and butter with a pastry cutter until you have pea-size pieces. Gently combine mixture with a little cold water. Add remaining water and gently roll the mixture around in the bowl to combine. Do not overwork the dough or the crust will be tough.

Wrap the pie crust with plastic wrap or place in a large ziplock bag and refrigerate for about 30 minutes to 1 hour.

Cut the dough into two equal-size pieces. Cover one piece with a clean towel or plastic wrap to keep it fresh. Roll out the other piece of dough on a lightly floured surface. Fold into quarters to easily lift the piece of dough into the pie plate, then open the folded dough to fill the plate; add pie filling.

Roll out the second piece of dough and place it over the filling. Press the top and bottom pieces of dough together to seal, rolling the dough under the edge of the pie plate, crimping as you go. Trim off any excess.

ICED TEA-LEMONADE

This refreshing summer mixture of iced tea and lemonade is perfect to quench your thirst. It's simple to brew your own tea, and nothing could be fresher. Growing up on a farm, this was a staple of summer refreshment for me.

Makes 1 gallon

2 CUPS GRANULATED SUGAR

JUICE OF 6 LARGE LEMONS

JUICE OF 2 LIMES

12 BLACK TEA BAGS

8 CUPS WATER

LEMON SLICES, FOR GARNISH

To a 1-gallon pouring pitcher or container, add the sugar, lemon juice, lime juice, and tea bags. Bring water to a boil and pour into the pitcher. Steep the tea bags in the pitcher for 20 to 30 minutes. Stir to combine, and fill pitcher with ice to cool. Pour into serving cups with ice, garnish with a slice of lemon, and enjoy.

RASPBERRY-OATMEAL BARS

We love traveling to Camden, Maine, because it's one of the prettiest and most relaxing seaside towns in New England. Camden Deli is a favorite spot of ours for evening coffee and dessert. These bars are a family favorite that my mom created based on the ones at the deli so that we could all get a sugary fix, even when we're not near Camden.

Makes 18 bars

1½ CUPS (3 STICKS) UNSALTED BUTTER, SOFTENED

2 CUPS FIRMLY PACKED BROWN SUGAR

3 CUPS ROLLED OATS

3 CUPS ALL-PURPOSE FLOUR

1 TEASPOON KOSHER SALT

1 TEASPOON BAKING POWDER

2 (12-OUNCE) JARS RASPBERRY PRESERVES

Preheat the oven to 350 degrees F. Grease a 9 x 13-inch baking pan with vegetable shortening or oil and set aside.

In a large mixing bowl, use a hand mixer to cream together butter and brown sugar until smooth. In a small bowl, combine the oats, flour, salt, and baking powder. Incorporate the dry ingredients into the creamed mixture, stirring to combine.

Press half of the mixture into the bottom of the baking pan. Spread the preserves over the crust in an even layer. Crumble the remaining crust mixture over the raspberry preserves layer. Bake for 45 to 50 minutes, or until lightly golden brown. Cool completely before cutting.

HERMIT COOKIES

Another staple in our French-Canadian household is this recipe from my father's mother, Helen Lamothe. This cookie is always a favorite at Christmastime. Use a shot glass or small round cookie cutter to cut out cookies.

Makes 3 dozen cookies

1 CUP (2 STICKS) UNSALTED BUTTER, SOFTENED

1 1/2 CUPS GRANULATED SUGAR

3 LARGE EGGS

1 CUP CHOPPED RAISINS OR CURRANTS

1 CUP CHOPPED DATES*

1 CUP CHOPPED WALNUTS

1 TEASPOON BAKING SODA

1 1/2 TEASPOONS WHITE VINEGAR

3 CUPS ALL-PURPOSE FLOUR

1 PINCH KOSHER SALT

1 TEASPOON GROUND CINNAMON

1/2 TEASPOON GROUND NUTMEG

Preheat the oven to 375 degrees F. Prepare a half sheet pan by lining it with parchment paper; set aside. In a mixing bowl, combine the butter, sugar, eggs, raisins, dates, and nuts. In a small bowl, mix the baking soda and vinegar; add to the sugar and egg mixture. Gradually add the flour, salt, cinnamon, and nutmeg. Stir until just combined.

On a lightly floured surface, use a rolling pin to roll out the dough to about 1/2 inch thick. Use a shot glass to cut out small cookies. Place cookies on the sheet pan and bake 10 to 12 minutes, or until golden.

*You can buy chopped dates. But if you chop dates or raisins in a food processor, be sure to add a little flour so they do not stick together. My mom cuts dates first with kitchen scissors before processing; otherwise it strains the food processor.

GRANDMA LAMOTHE'S MEAT PIE

My French-Canadian grandmother was born in Canada, then later moved to Berlin, New Hampshire. She always made this delectable meat pie for the holidays. She said it could be served with a turkey for Thanksgiving in place of stuffing. My father, brother, and husband always save plenty of room for this amazing pie!

Serves 4 to 6

PIE CRUST (PAGE 20)

¾ CUP FINELY DICED CELERY

½ CUP FINELY DICED ONION

6 CUPS WATER

2 POUNDS GROUND BEEF ROUND

2 POUNDS GROUND PORK

2 TEASPOONS KOSHER SALT

2 TEASPOONS FRESHLY GROUND BLACK PEPPER

1 TEASPOON POULTRY SEASONING

½ TEASPOON DRIED PARSLEY

2 CUPS UNSEASONED BREADCRUMBS

¼ TEASPOON GROUND CLOVES

Preheat the oven to 375 degrees F. Fit a layer of pie crust dough into a 9-inch pie pan and set aside.

In a large pot, add the celery, onion, water, beef, pork, salt, pepper, and poultry seasoning; cook over medium heat. When the meat is cooked and the vegetables are tender, about 20 minutes, add breadcrumbs and cloves. Add the meat mixture to the unbaked pie crust. Cover with the top layer of pie crust dough, crimping the edges and cutting a few ventilation holes with a sharp knife. Bake for approximately 45 minutes, or until the crust is golden brown. Let cool for 10 minutes and serve.

ROGERS ORCHARDS

CORN PEACHES

MACOUNS

A FRUITFUL HARVEST

ORCHARDS, HONEY &
LOCAL FARM STANDS

One morning before school, a few horses from the barn across the way got loose. I think we were all shocked to discover that they were in our backyard, feasting on the harvest from our one and only apple tree. My brother's friend went into her backyard and picked a bunch of carrots for the horses out of her family's garden.

The horses aren't the only ones tempted by New England's bounty. In the spring, summer, and fall, berries, peaches, apples, pears, and pumpkins are ripe for the picking in many locations throughout New England. The warmth of spring and summer plumps strawberries and raspberries, but as soon as the crisp autumn air hits my skin, I know it's time to visit local orchards for freshly harvested apples, winter squash, and pumpkins. We drive throughout New England during the fall to absorb all the brilliant colors Mother Nature created and the simple pleasures of the autumn season.

Enjoy a ride on a hay-filled wagon at one of the local farms in New England to select the perfect pumpkin. Or pick the crispest fresh apples right off the tree. If you don't want to pick the fruit yourself, many of the farms have done the work for you. Their farm stands offer freshly harvested fruits, veggies, and farm-made products. It simply couldn't be fresher. Buying local ensures that you are getting the freshest produce possible and reducing fossil fuel consumption, all while supporting your local farmer.

In the winter, trudge through the newly fallen snow and pick out a fragrant Christmas tree that the entire family can enjoy. There is nothing quite like having a fresh evergreen in your home, bringing nature indoors and intense life to your living room. Don't forget to pick up a handmade wreath for your front door at the same farm! You can also create your own handmade wreath with fresh evergreens.

✦ **RICKER HILL ORCHARDS**, in Turner, Maine, offers a wonderful selection of locally grown produce, including 40 different varieties of apples, fresh cranberries, and many baked goods. The family-run orchard has been growing apples since 1803 and is now in its tenth generation of operation. One of my favorite features of the orchard is their charming country gift store and bakery, where you can pick up everything from farm-made jams, freshly baked apple pies, maple syrup, local honey, and Vermont-made wooden toys. They also offer freshly harvested Maine-grown Christmas trees and wreaths during the holiday season. The farm has an entertaining play yard for the kids, featuring a corn box to dig in, hay bale and corn mazes, bounce houses, and miniature golf. Our kids love this farm and orchard as much we love their wonderful fresh apples and farm-fresh produce.

Through meticulous research around New England, here's a guide to the best orchards and their farm stand offerings:

✦ **ALYSON'S ORCHARD** in Walpole, New Hampshire, is a 500-acre working orchard. Their family-run farm is one of the finest heirloom apple orchards in New England. They produce 50 varieties of apples along with berries, grapes, peaches, plums, and pears. Their attractive farm stand is open early summer to late fall and offers a tempting selection of fresh produce, freshly baked pies, unpasteurized apple cider and their own farm-made fruit wines. They are also available to host your wedding or special event in their beautiful Orchard Room, which can comfortably seat up to 250 guests. Alyson's also offers three different lodging sites for your weekend getaway in any season. During the summer, you can go camping, canoeing, hiking, fishing, or swimming; in the winter you can ski the slopes nearby.

✦ **VERRILL FARM** sits in the historic town of Concord, Massachusetts. The farm stand is beautiful and was recently renovated. The farm originally started as a dairy farm and now has a greenhouse and working bakery, offering prepared foods and freshly harvested produce. Their impressive store is spacious, clean, and stocked full of rustic baskets filled daily with incredible produce. Refrigerated coolers line back walls with locally made ice creams, eggs, dairy items, pies, and more.

✦ **APPLECREST FARM** in Hampton Falls, New Hampshire, is the oldest and largest apple orchard in New Hampshire, as well as the oldest continuously operated orchard in the United States. Their farm store is situated in a rustic 200-year-old barn. Here you will find all the goodies of New England, including freshly pressed apple cider, sweet corn, berries, seasonal vegetables, milk in glass bottles, and hot apple cider donuts. Their farm store is open seven days a week, May through December.

✦ **AVERILL FARM,** in the quiet town of Washington Depot, Connecticut, has for many years operated as a dairy farm. Drive down a winding and narrow gray pebble driveway to their quaint farm stand set in the heart of the apple orchard. Today the farm grows 86 different varieties of apples on the 250-acre property. The farm is now in its ninth generation of operation, a legacy that began in 1746. Susan Averill fills their farm stand with homemade jams, jellies, donuts, and other locally produced products such as maple syrup and honey. Bring the kids in October to select the perfectly ripe pumpkin for their jack-o-lanterns or for making homemade pumpkin pie. The farm also offers cut-your-own Christmas trees, specializing in fragrant blue spruce, white spruce, and firs.

✦ **BELLTOWN HILL ORCHARDS** in South Glastonbury, Connecticut, is one of the prettiest farm stands and orchards in Connecticut. As you drive into the narrow driveway and park your car, the serene views of the orchard will take your breath away. You can either pick your own or purchase fruits that are already harvested inside their adorable farm store. Handmade goat milk soaps, wool yarn, farm-made jams, and other confections are all offered in their beautiful, manicured store. You'll also find refrigerated coolers filled with locally made ice cream, eggs, pies, and cheeses.

✦ **BARDEN FAMILY ORCHARD**, situated in North Scituate, Rhode Island, has been in operation since 1931 with a dark rooster-red building and covered porch overlooking the farm. Their farm store has a very spacious feel with its high ceilings and earthy, exposed natural wood beams. They are open July through Thanksgiving and offer an assortment of beautiful vegetables, fruit, pumpkins, and mums. You'll also find a large selection of jams, jellies, baking mixes, and locally made cheeses. The orchard offers a great selection of apples and their own apple cider.

✦ **THE APPLE BARN** in Bennington, Vermont, has a stunning deep-red barn with white painted trim and a pebble pathway to the entrance. The farm stand is beautifully landscaped and full of Vermont-made products. Wooden shelves and farmhouse style tables are stocked full of jams, jellies, applesauce, and baking mixes. You can schedule a tour of their farm, which sits high above the 300-acre apple orchard.

✦ **COLD HOLLOW CIDER MILL** in Waterbury Center is one of Vermont's largest cider mills. They press cider the old-fashioned way with a traditional rack-and-cloth press that was built in the early 1920s. During the fall, watch apple cider being pressed, or in the summer observe the frolicking bees making honey. Be sure to visit their gift shop for all of Vermont's finest confections, like an array of incredible preserves.

✦ **KARABIN FARM,** located on the back roads of Southington, Connecticut, is a family-run farm with a petting zoo, where you can cut your own Christmas trees and pick your own fruits as well as purchase their pure maple syrup. Diane Karabin and her sister make sure their country-style farm store is fully stocked with a wide array of specialty foods, produce, and handcrafted rustic furniture. They are one of the best farms in Connecticut to visit for the highest-quality annuals and amazing hanging baskets grown right in their own greenhouses, with a unique twist offered up each growing season. Their farm stand also offers a wide variety of locally made jams, honey, and cheeses along with country furniture. Grab one of their Radio Flyer wagons and tour the farm with the kids. During the fall, visit their farm for the freshest crisp apples and delicious apple cider donuts made right at their farm. During the holiday season, walk the fields to harvest the freshest-smelling Christmas tree. Stop by the store and bring home a stunning poinsettia or pick from a wonderful selection of handmade gifts.

✦ **SCHARTNER FARMS** in Exeter, Rhode Island, sits on 150 acres of pristine farmland dating back to 1902. They offer a wide variety of locally grown produce, baked goods, gourmet foods, and preserves. The farm originally produced bulk potatoes for Wise and Frito-Lay until the retail stand opened in 1972. If you want to tempt your taste buds, don't miss the deli, which offers homemade soups, sandwiches, and salads. When in season, pick-your-own strawberries and blueberries are available.

✦ **ROGERS ORCHARDS** in Southington, Connecticut, began 200 years ago. Their open-air-style markets are rustic with concrete floors and shelves filled with all you'll ever need (plus the smells of sweet produce heaven grace your nose as you walk into the store). Now with two locations, they offer a wide variety of farm-made pies, apple coffee cake, and incredible freshly harvested fruits. They grow 26 different varieties of apples, along with peaches, pears, nectarines, and sweet corn. People wait in line for fresh, hot apple cider donuts rolled in granular sugar on a busy weekend during the fall. The farm also offers local honey, maple syrup from Connecticut and Vermont, and their own private label jams and jellies. The Sunnymount location offers a duck pond for the kids to visit and breathtaking views that overlook the mountains.

✦ **ROSE'S BERRY FARM** has been farming the hills of South Glastonbury, Connecticut, for 100 years, striving to produce the finest berries in Connecticut on more than 100 acres of land. Weather permitting, Rose's Berry Farm is one of the best places to have Sunday brunch. During their harvest season, sit outside to absorb tremendous views and sample traditional breakfast food, all served with the farm's freshest berries. They offer pick-your-own baskets for fruits and berries such as apples, blueberries, raspberries, and pumpkins, or you can purchase fruit, jams, pies, and other homemade treats in their farm store.

✦ **BARDEN FAMILY ORCHARD** has been picking farm-fresh produce since 1931 in North Scituate, Rhode Island. Walk into their new farm market to find freshly picked fruits, vegetables, and other items such as jams and maple syrup. If you can't venture to their farm, don't worry; you can locate their produce and products at one of the many farmers markets. Not only do they have the very best apples—many different varieties to satisfy everyone's palate—but there are also freshly picked sweet corn, raspberries, nectarines, and a variety of squash.

✦ **COOK'S FARM ORCHARD** in Brimfield, Massachusetts, is a fascinating farm and a great excuse to experience summer or autumn at an authentic old-fashioned New England family farm. With their stand situated in a rustic New England barn, the summer offerings include blueberries, apples, fruit preserves, farm-made applesauce, homemade pies, and baked goods. In the fall, their farm is filled with plump orange pumpkins, and fall festivals bring a petting zoo, wagon rides, and a hay maze.

✦ **BARTLETT'S APPLE ORCHARD** in Richmond, Massachusetts, has been plucking the juiciest apples from their trees since 1947. The farm stand is open 7 days a week year-round, offering 18 different varieties of apples grown right on their farm. Bring your family to watch cider being pressed and take home a gallon to enjoy later, or sip spiced hot cider and soak in the aromas of the crisp autumn air. Their country store boasts locally made items like jams, jellies, fudge, maple syrup, natural peanut butter, and other wonderful New England–made specialties. You can also pick up local fresh eggs, milk, and ice cream.

EVERYTHING YOU NEED TO KNOW ABOUT HONEY

Andrew's Local Honey, located in Norwalk, Connecticut, has been producing honey since the late 1800s. Andrew's honey is 100% pure, raw, local, and kosher, and their vast array of honey products—honey, bee pollen, honeycomb, and more—are found at local farmers markets and in specialty food stores. But if you buy the finest in honey, make sure you know how to use and keep it fresh.

Never refrigerate honey. Should the honey crystallize, simply boil a small pot of water, shut the burner off, and set the container of honey into the hot water.

Honey should not be fed to infants less than one year of age. Honey is safe for older children and adults.

Locally produced honey can combat seasonal allergies since your body builds immunity to area plants that you would otherwise be allergic to. If you are using honey to combat allergies, be sure not to put the honey into anything hot, as it will kill the natural enzymes and bacteria that are good for you. Another way to combat seasonal allergies is with bee pollen; collected by the bees, it is three times more powerful than honey.

Honeybees are actually European in origin and were transported to North America along with the earliest settlers.

Bees collect 66 pounds of pollen per year, per hive; they also account for 80 percent of all insect pollination. If not for the honeybee transferring pollen from one flower to another, many of our foods simply would not grow and develop.

RUSTIC BERRY TART

This tart will melt in your mouth and is the perfect addition to any gathering. It can be made as one large tart or individual petite tarts to serve at a party, so each person can have their own dessert. You can make the dough ahead of time and refrigerate. Just be careful not to overwork the dough.

Serves 6 to 8

FOR THE CRUST:

1 1/4 CUPS ALL-PURPOSE FLOUR

2 TABLESPOONS GRANULATED SUGAR

1/4 TEASPOON KOSHER SALT

1/2 CUP (1 STICK) UNSALTED BUTTER, CHILLED

4 OUNCES CREAM CHEESE, CHILLED AND CUT INTO 1/2-INCH PIECES

2 TEASPOONS FRESHLY SQUEEZED LEMON JUICE

1 TO 2 TABLESPOONS ICE WATER

FOR THE FILLING:

2 PINTS (4 CUPS) BLUEBERRIES, WASHED AND PATTED DRY

2 PINTS (4 CUPS) RASPBERRIES, WASHED AND PATTED DRY

2 TABLESPOONS SMALL PEARL TAPIOCA

1 TABLESPOON FRESHLY SQUEEZED LEMON JUICE

1/4 CUP GRANULATED SUGAR, PLUS MORE FOR SPRINKLING

1 LARGE EGG, BEATEN

HOMEMADE WHIPPED CREAM, FOR SERVING (OPTIONAL)

Preheat the oven to 400 degrees F. Line a half baking sheet with parchment paper and set aside.

In a large bowl, add the flour, sugar, and salt, stirring to combine. Cut the butter and cream cheese into the flour with a fork until mixture resembles small peas, without overworking the dough. Sprinkle the lemon juice and 1 tablespoon water over mixture. Use your hands to fold the dough, thoroughly mixing in liquid until dough holds together when squeezed. Add a little more cold water if necessary (just enough to bring the dough together). The dough will be slightly sticky. Turn dough onto a lightly floured work surface and gather into a ball. Flatten into a round disk and wrap in plastic wrap. Refrigerate dough for at least 30 minutes.

Using a knife, cut the dough into 6 equal-size wedges. On a lightly floured surface, roll each section of dough into a circle. Place dough circles on the baking sheet. In a medium bowl, combine the berries, tapioca, lemon juice, and 1/4 cup sugar. Place a few spoonfuls of the berry mixture inside each circle. Fold in the dough towards the center, pinching it.

Brush the tart crusts with the beaten egg and sprinkle with sugar. Bake until crust is lightly golden brown, about 30 to 35 minutes. Cool on a baking rack for about 10 minutes. Serve with whipped cream.

OATMEAL RAISIN FILLED BAKED APPLES

Coming from a family who always had to serve dessert, these are a simple yet tasty treat. My mom made these yummy flavorful treats every fall for apple harvest season. The autumn spices will make you want a second helping.

Serves 6

6 LARGE APPLES

2 CUPS ROLLED OATS

½ CUP RAISINS

½ TEASPOON CINNAMON

½ CUP GRANULATED MAPLE SUGAR

½ CUP FIRMLY PACKED BROWN SUGAR

¼ CUP CHOPPED PECANS (OPTIONAL)

VANILLA ICE CREAM, FOR SERVING (OPTIONAL)

Preheat the oven to 375 degrees F.

Wash and core the apples, making sure not to break through the bottom. Place apples in an oven-safe baking dish.

In a medium bowl, add the oats, raisins, cinnamon, maple sugar, brown sugar, and pecans. Mix together. Scoop filling into the centers of the apples. Bake for 30 minutes, or until the sugar is bubbly. Serve warm with ice cream.

STRAWBERRY-TOPPED CHEESECAKE

Ever since I can remember, my mother was a genius in the kitchen. She was always baking breads, cakes, homemade pizza, and more—all from scratch. My mother has made this cheesecake for years. It has a wonderfully creamy texture and is simply delicious.

Serves 6 to 8

FOR THE CHEESECAKE:

12 OUNCES CREAM CHEESE, SOFTENED

¾ CUP GRANULATED SUGAR

2 LARGE EGGS

1 CUP SOUR CREAM

½ CUP HEAVY CREAM

½ TEASPOON PURE VANILLA EXTRACT

2 TEASPOONS FRESHLY SQUEEZED LEMON JUICE

FOR THE GRAHAM CRACKER CRUST:

1 (13.5-OUNCE) PACKAGE GRAHAM CRACKER CRUMBS

⅔ CUP MELTED BUTTER

½ CUP GRANULATED SUGAR

FOR THE FRUIT TOPPING:

2 CUPS FROZEN SLICED STRAWBERRIES WITH SUGAR

1 (3.4-OUNCE) PACKAGE STRAWBERRY JELL-O

¾ CUP STRAWBERRY JAM

Preheat the oven to 350 degrees F.

In a large bowl, use a spatula to mix together the cream cheese and sugar. Add the eggs one at a time and combine. Add in the sour cream, heavy cream, vanilla, and lemon juice and mix thoroughly to incorporate.

In a small bowl, combine the graham cracker crumbs, butter, and sugar. Pat the crumb mixture into the bottom of a 9-inch springform pan. Pour the cheesecake mixture into the pan and bake for 1 hour. After 1 hour, turn off the oven. Leave the cheesecake in the oven for 2 hours, making certain not to open the oven during this time.

In a medium saucepan over low to medium heat, add the strawberries, Jell-O, and jam, and cook for about 10 minutes, stirring frequently, until berry mixture is thickened. Carefully transfer mixture to a food processor, and purée. Cool mixture to room temperature. After the 2-hour mark, remove the cheesecake from the oven and remove the top portion of the pan. Top cheesecake with the strawberry mixture, and refrigerate until ready to serve.

Variation: Substitute 2 cups whole raspberries and raspberry Jell-O for the frozen strawberries and strawberry Jell-O. You can use raspberry jam or mix raspberry and strawberry for more flavor.

APPLE STREUSEL CAKE

Warm cinnamon and freshly harvested apples in this wonderfully moist cake will leave you wanting more. Look at your local orchard for an apple that's in season, tart, and bakes well.

Serves 6 to 8

FOR THE STREUSEL:

1 CUP FIRMLY PACKED BROWN SUGAR

1 CUP CORED, PEELED, AND CHOPPED APPLES

1 CUP CHOPPED PECANS (OPTIONAL)

¼ CUP ALL-PURPOSE FLOUR

1 TEASPOON GROUND CINNAMON

½ TEASPOON GROUND NUTMEG

3 TABLESPOONS UNSALTED BUTTER, MELTED

FOR THE CAKE:

2 CUPS ALL-PURPOSE FLOUR

1 TEASPOON BAKING POWDER

1 TEASPOON BAKING SODA

½ CUP (1 STICK) UNSALTED BUTTER, SOFTENED

½ CUP GRANULATED SUGAR

3 LARGE EGGS

1 TEASPOON PURE VANILLA EXTRACT

½ CUP PLAIN YOGURT

FOR THE GLAZE:

2 CUPS CONFECTIONERS' SUGAR

1 TEASPOON VANILLA EXTRACT

2–3 TABLESPOONS MILK

Preheat the oven to 350 degrees F. Using a pastry brush, grease a 9- or 10-inch tube pan or a Bundt pan with vegetable shortening and set aside.

To make the streusel, in a medium bowl add the brown sugar, apples, pecans, flour, cinnamon, and nutmeg. Stir to combine. Pour in the melted butter, using a fork to incorporate it with the other ingredients. Set aside.

To make the cake, in a medium bowl add the flour, baking powder, and baking soda, mixing together to combine. In a large bowl, add the butter and sugar, using a hand mixer to cream mixture together until light and fluffy, about 6 to 7 minutes. Add the eggs, one at a time, mixing after each egg is added. Add the vanilla and stir to combine. Alternate adding the yogurt and the flour mixture into the cake batter, mixing together on low speed. Pour half the batter into the prepared pan, and then sprinkle half the streusel over the batter. Top with the remaining cake batter, and use a butter knife to swirl batter and streusel together to create a marble pattern. (Be careful not to touch the bottom of the pan with the knife or pan will scratch.) Bake for 15 minutes. Remove cake and sprinkle remaining streusel mixture evenly over the top. Return cake to oven and bake 30 to 35 minutes, or until a toothpick inserted into the center comes out clean. Remove cake from the oven and allow to cool on a wire rack.

Make the glaze by whisking together the sugar, vanilla, and milk in a medium bowl. Drizzle over the cooled cake and serve.

CRANBERRY-ORANGE SCONES

Cranberries are an important piece of our New England heritage. Native Americans were the first to find the berry and realize its versatile uses. Today, farmers in the United States grow more than 40,000 acres of cranberries. The mix of orange and cranberries in this scone will tempt your every taste bud and are perfect for breakfast or afternoon tea.

Makes 12 scones

2¾ CUPS ALL-PURPOSE FLOUR

¼ CUP GRANULATED SUGAR

1 TEASPOON KOSHER SALT

1 TABLESPOON BAKING POWDER

½ CUP (1 STICK) UNSALTED BUTTER, VERY COLD

2 LARGE EGGS

2 TEASPOONS PURE ORANGE OIL

ZEST OF 1 ORANGE

⅔ CUP BUTTERMILK

1 CUP DRIED CRANBERRIES

HEAVY CREAM

SUGAR CRYSTALS

Line a sheet pan with parchment paper and set aside.

In a large bowl, whisk together the flour, sugar, salt, and baking powder. Put the bowl into the freezer for about 30 minutes to chill the flour mixture. Using a stand mixer, add the cold butter to the dry ingredients and mix just until crumbly. In a separate measuring cup or bowl, whisk together the eggs and orange oil. Add the liquid ingredients to the dry ingredients and stir until everything is moistened and holds together. Gently fold in the dried cranberries.

Turn dough out onto a lightly floured surface and flatten down with your hands. Place dough in a plastic bag and refrigerate for 3 to 4 hours. Turn the dough out onto a lightly floured surface, and roll it out into a rectangle shape about ¾ inch thick. Cut diagonally to make triangles. Place the triangle-shaped scones onto the prepared sheet pan, leaving a little bit of space between them. Place the scones in the freezer for 1 to 2 hours. You can freeze scones for up to 2 weeks, until you are ready to bake them.

Preheat the oven to 425 degrees F. Brush the scones with heavy cream and sprinkle with sugar crystals. Bake for 20 to 25 minutes, or until golden brown. They should not be soft when you press on the centers. Let the scones cool on a baking rack for 5 to 10 minutes. Enjoy warm or allow to cool completely before putting into a plastic bag for storage.

YELLOW CAKE WITH MIXED BERRY JAM

This is a cake recipe I developed in the commercial kitchen of my family's sugar house. We had just started hosting farm-to-table dinners for our wholesale customers, and I decided to make mini desserts for the occasions. While I created the mixed berry jam recipe for the sugar house, I wanted to merge it into a recipe for spring or summer entertaining.

Serves 6 to 8

FOR THE CAKE:

2¾ CUPS ALL-PURPOSE FLOUR

1 TEASPOON KOSHER SALT

2½ TEASPOONS BAKING POWDER

¾ CUP (1½ STICKS) UNSALTED BUTTER, SOFTENED

1 CUP GRANULATED SUGAR

¾ CUP GRANULATED MAPLE SUGAR

2 TEASPOONS PURE VANILLA EXTRACT

5 LARGE EGGS

1½ CUPS HALF-AND-HALF

1 12-OUNCE JAR MIXED BERRY JAM (SEE PAGE 131)

FOR THE ICING:

1½ CUPS CONFECTIONERS' SUGAR

1 TABLESPOON FRESHLY SQUEEZED LEMON JUICE

2 TABLESPOONS WHOLE MILK

Preheat the oven to 350 degrees F. Spray a large Bundt pan with cooking spray and set aside. Line a baking sheet with parchment paper and set aside.

In a large bowl, stir together the flour, salt, and baking powder; set aside. In another large bowl, use a hand mixer to cream together the butter, granulated sugar, maple sugar, and vanilla on low speed until mixture is fluffy, 4 to 5 minutes. Add the eggs to the creamed sugar one at a time. Alternately add the flour mixture and the half-and-half to the sugar and egg mixture, using a spatula to scrape the sides of the bowl so all the ingredients are combined.

Pour all of the cake batter into the pan, which should be about three-fourths full. Using a spoon, add spoonfuls of jam to the top of the uncooked cake. Place the Bundt pan onto a parchment paper–lined baking sheet. Bake cake for 55 to 60 minutes, or until a toothpick inserted into the center of the cake comes out clean. Remove the cake from the oven and allow to cool in the pan for 5 minutes. Flip the pan over onto the baking rack, remove the cake from the pan, and allow cake to cool completely.

In a medium bowl, add the confectioners' sugar, lemon juice, and milk. Use a whisk to stir until a paste is formed. Drizzle the cooled cake with icing and enjoy.

SWEET & TANGY APPLE CIDER BARBEQUE SAUCE

This sauce is perfect over a pork roast or beef brisket for sandwiches. Making homemade barbeque sauce lets you control the ingredients. You'll be amazed at how simple it is to make, as well as how flavorful it turns out.

Makes 3 cups

½ CUP TOMATO PASTE

¾ CUP CIDER VINEGAR

½ CUP APPLE CIDER

½ CUP MOLASSES

½ CUP FIRMLY PACKED BROWN SUGAR

½ CUP HONEY

⅔ CUP GRANULATED SUGAR

1 TABLESPOON GRANULATED ONION

1 TABLESPOON GROUND MUSTARD POWDER

¼ TEASPOON SMOKED PAPRIKA

¼ TEASPOON KOSHER SALT

¼ TEASPOON FRESHLY GROUND BLACK PEPPER

½ TEASPOON GROUND CAYENNE PEPPER

In a medium pot over medium heat, add the tomato paste, vinegar, and cider, whisking to combine. Add the molasses, brown sugar, honey, granulated sugar, granulated onion, mustard powder, paprika, salt, black pepper, and cayenne, whisking to combine. Bring to a boil, reduce the heat to low, and simmer until desired thickness is achieved, stirring occasionally with a wooden spoon. To check the thickness, spoon a little bit of sauce into a small measuring cup, put it in the freezer for a few minutes, and taste.

SPICED PUMPKIN CUPCAKES

Autumn is one of my favorite seasons. It's time to visit local fairs, enjoy clam chowder, sip hot cider, and soak in the autumn foliage. Of course, the season wouldn't be complete without a trip to one of our local farms to pick some pumpkins. This is one of the moistest spiced pumpkin cupcakes you'll ever have. Using a pinch of salt in sweet recipes, like the cupcakes and frosting, heightens the sweetness.

Makes 30 cupcakes

FOR THE PUMPKIN CUPCAKES:

4 LARGE EGGS

¾ CUP SHORTENING

2 CUPS GRANULATED SUGAR

2 CUPS MASHED PUMPKIN

1 CUP WHOLE YOGURT

1 TEASPOON PURE VANILLA EXTRACT

2½ CUPS ALL-PURPOSE FLOUR

2 TEASPOONS BAKING POWDER

1 TEASPOON BAKING SODA

1 TEASPOON KOSHER SALT

1½ TEASPOONS CINNAMON

½ TEASPOON GROUND NUTMEG

FOR THE CREAM CHEESE FROSTING:

1 (8-OUNCE) PACKAGE CREAM CHEESE, SOFTENED

¾ CUP SHORTENING

4 CUPS CONFECTIONERS' SUGAR

2 TEASPOONS PURE VANILLA EXTRACT

½ TEASPOON KOSHER SALT

¼ CUP HALF-AND-HALF

Preheat the oven to 350 degrees F. Line muffin pans with paper liners and set aside.

In a large bowl, add the eggs, shortening, sugar, pumpkin, yogurt, and vanilla. Mix with a spatula to combine. In a separate large bowl, combine the flour, baking powder, baking soda, salt, cinnamon, and nutmeg. Slowly add the dry ingredients to the pumpkin mixture, stirring to combine well. Divide batter evenly among muffin cups, filling each cup about two-thirds full. Bake (in batches if need be) until a toothpick inserted in the center comes out clean, about 25 minutes. Remove from oven and allow to cool completely before frosting.

In the bowl of a stand mixer, add the cream cheese, shortening, and confectioners' sugar. Beat until fluffy, 6 to 8 minutes. Add the vanilla, salt, and half-and-half; continue to mix just until incorporated and smooth. Frost cooled cupcakes and serve.

JALAPEÑO CHILI

Chili is wonderfully satisfying any cool night, especially during the fall or winter. I often will order Italian bread bowls from our local bakery to serve the chili in. Top it off with freshly shredded Vermont cheddar cheese and enjoy. Add jalapeño bacon from your local butcher to give it a little extra kick.

Serves 8

3 POUNDS 80% LEAN GROUND CHUCK

½ POUND JALAPEÑO BACON, FINELY CHOPPED

1 LARGE ONION, FINELY CHOPPED

1 LARGE GREEN PEPPER, FINELY CHOPPED

2 CUPS APPLE CIDER

2 CUPS BEEF STOCK

1 (15-OUNCE) CONTAINER FRESH SALSA VERDE

2 (15-OUNCE) CANS BEANS, DRAINED (BLACK BEANS, KIDNEY BEANS, OR ONE OF EACH)

2 BEEF BOUILLON CUBES

1 TABLESPOON GROUND SMOKED PAPRIKA

1 TABLESPOON GROUND CHILI POWDER

SALT AND FRESHLY GROUND BLACK PEPPER

SHREDDED CHEDDAR CHEESE, FOR SERVING

In a large heavy-duty pot, cook the ground chuck over medium-high heat until browned, 8 to 10 minutes, stirring with a spatula to break the meat up. Remove the meat from the pot and reserve. Add the bacon, onion, and pepper to the pot, cooking over medium-high heat until the bacon is crispy, about 10 minutes. Add reserved beef to the pot, along with the cider, stock, salsa verde, beans, bouillon cubes, paprika, and chili powder. Season to taste with salt and pepper. Stir with a wooden spoon to combine. Reduce heat to low, and allow the chili to simmer for about 1 hour. Serve topped with cheddar cheese.

BRIOCHE STICKY BUNS

This brioche dough isn't just for sticky buns: it can also be rolled out and cut into strips with added chocolate pieces or raspberry filling for wonderful breakfast pastries. This yummy French dough is relatively simple to make and boasts a super flakey and buttery texture.

Makes 18 to 20 brioche buns

FOR THE BRIOCHE:

6 CUPS ALL-PURPOSE FLOUR

1/2 CUP GRANULATED SUGAR

1 1/2 TABLESPOONS ACTIVE DRY YEAST

1 TEASPOON KOSHER SALT

5 LARGE EGGS, AT ROOM TEMPERATURE

1 1/4 CUP WHOLE MILK, WARM (115 DEGREES F)

1 CUP (2 STICKS) UNSALTED BUTTER, SLIGHTLY SOFTENED AND CUT INTO PIECES

FOR THE CARAMEL SAUCE:

1 CUP (2 STICKS) UNSALTED BUTTER

2 CUPS FIRMLY PACKED BROWN SUGAR

1 CUP CORN SYRUP

1 (14-OUNCE) CAN SWEETENED CONDENSED MILK

1 TEASPOON PURE VANILLA EXTRACT

FOR THE CINNAMON-SUGAR FILLING:

2 CUPS FIRMLY PACKED BROWN SUGAR

1 CUP (2 STICKS) BUTTER, MELTED

2 TEASPOONS CINNAMON

1/2 CUP CHOPPED PECANS, PLUS EXTRA FOR SPRINKLING

To make the brioche, in the bowl of a stand mixer with a mixer attachment combine the flour, sugar, yeast, and salt. Add the eggs and the milk. With a spatula, scrape the bowl to thoroughly combine the ingredients. Change the attachment to the dough hook; mix for about 2 minutes. With the mixer on medium speed, add 1/2 cup butter. Scrape down the bowl and dough hook, and continue to mix for about 4 minutes, until the butter is incorporated. Add the remaining 1/2 cup butter and continue to mix for another 4 minutes or so. Scrape the bowl and dough hook again. Mix until the dough is smooth, shiny, and soft, about another 4 minutes. (The dough may look sticky and loose at this point, but resist the urge to add more flour, or your brioche may become tough.) Turn the dough out onto a lightly floured surface and knead a few times by hand to form a ball. Grease the mixing bowl with butter and place the dough back in the bowl. Cover loosely with plastic wrap. Let the dough rise until doubled, about 1 hour.

Turn the dough out onto a lightly floured surface and knead by hand a few times. Place the dough back in the mixing bowl with smooth side up. Cover with plastic wrap and let rise for an additional 1 hour, until doubled in size.

To make the caramel sauce, in a medium saucepan melt the butter, brown sugar, and corn syrup over medium heat. Once melted, add the condensed milk. Cook for 10 to 15 minutes, just until it comes to a boil, stirring occasionally with a wooden spoon to keep the sauce from burning. Remove from the heat and stir in the vanilla.

To make the cinnamon-sugar filling, mix together the brown sugar, butter, cinnamon, and pecans in a medium bowl.

To make the buns, prepare two half baking sheets or a 9 x 13-inch pan by brushing with softened butter. Pour the caramel sauce into each pan, just enough to cover the bottom. Sprinkle with a handful or two of pecan pieces.

Cut the dough in half. Place half the dough back in the bowl and cover with plastic wrap. With a wooden rolling pin, roll out the other half on a lightly floured surface into a rectangle shape, about 12 x 18 inches and $1/4$ inch thick. Spread half of the cinnamon-sugar filling on the dough. Roll the dough up from long side. Cut into about 2-inch pieces and place in the prepared pans, leaving enough space between them for the rolls to rise. Repeat the same process with the remaining half of the dough. Cover the pans with plastic wrap and refrigerate overnight.

Preheat the oven to 375 degrees F. Meanwhile, let the buns rise on the counter for about 1 hour. Bake the sticky buns for 30 to 35 minutes, or until golden brown. Remove the pan from the oven and immediately invert onto a serving plate. Allow to cool for a few minutes and serve warm.

Raspberry Greek
Yogurt

Produced and Packaged by
WWW.HastingsFamilyFarm.com

472 Hill street
Suffield CT
860-668-7524

HASTINGS
FARM LLC

8 oz

JUL 1 5 2013

Sell By

Grade A All Natural Cream Line Milk
(We do not use Artificial Growth Hormones)
472 Hill street Suffield CT 860-668-7524
WWW.HastingsFamilyFarm.com
Produced and Packaged by

HALF GALLON

HASTINGS
FARM LLC

Sell By: 7/4

7 00220 02592 9

RICH & DELICIOUS

EGGS, CHEESES &

DAIRY PRODUCTS

When I was a little girl, my family helped the dairy farm down the road with activities like baling hay from their fields or anything else they needed. In return, Mrs. Pavlick sent milk home with my dad each week, packing the milk in recycled Tropicana glass bottles. It was the type of milk that needed to be shaken before you poured it—oh, the creaminess and how wonderfully rich it tasted! I have to say, we became spoiled having daily fresh milk. We knew that the milk was the freshest it could be, traveling straight from the cows to our kitchen.

New England has a slice of the best dairy and poultry farms that are still in operation. Many of these have gone back to basics to produce healthy dairy products that are naturally free of chemicals, hormones, and preservatives. When you use fresh ingredients in your baking and cooking, the difference is tremendous and scrumptious. Start with only the freshest ingredients and the end result will be remarkable.

Lately, there has been a big push for raw milk. It's often said that raw milk, which is unpasteurized and non-homogenized, is more nutritious and can also help people who suffer from eczema and allergies. While there may be a wealth of health benefits to consuming raw milk, health professionals urge families to use caution because raw milk can harbor dangerous microorganisms that can pose health risks. In many states, you can only buy raw milk directly from the farm that produced it. There is also milk that has been pasteurized but not homogenized, the process that breaks up the fat into smaller particles so the milk no longer separates. Milk that has not been homogenized simply needs to be shaken before pouring.

✦ ARETHUSA FARMS, located in the hills of Litchfield, Connecticut, produces and bottles probably one of the best-tasting milks I've ever had the pleasure to drink. The farm prides itself on their attention to detail and production of high-quality products. Their cows are treated like royalty, and the farm goes out of their way to make sure every effort is made for cleanliness. They have a wonderful retail store only minutes down the road, in Bantam, Connecticut, called ARETHUSA FARM DAIRY. Treat yourself by purchasing their flavorful milk, cream, and yogurts at their farm store or in many specialty food stores throughout Connecticut.

+ **HASTINGS FAMILY FARM** in Suffield, Connecticut, has the best milk! I fell in love with it a few years ago. Megan and her husband Dan can be found at a few select farmers markets on the weekend. Or, during the week, Megan will be bottling milk, packaging Greek-style yogurt, or creating a new flavor of soft cheese at the farm's bottling facility. Their milk is pasteurized but not homogenized, which means the cream naturally floats to the top and needs to be shaken before pouring. Their farm store offers coolers of fresh whole milk and chocolate milk in half-gallons as well as individual serving bottles. The store is simple, clean, and packed with milk, cheeses, free-range eggs, and cuts of beef.

+ **THE FARMER'S COW** in Lebanon, Connecticut, is comprised of six family-owned dairy farms. After people kept asking, "Where can we buy your milk?" they decided to form their own company to sell their products throughout Southern New England and New York. They offer a selection of farm-fresh milk, eggs, heavy cream, half-and-half, apple cider, and The Farmer's Daughter summertime beverages, which includes one of my personal favorites, an iced tea-lemonade combo. Ice cream has also been recently added to their incredible product line. Because their milk is locally produced, bottled fresh, and has no hormones, it translates into an amazing ice cream.

+ **SMYTH'S TRINITY FARMS,** in Enfield, Connecticut, still bottles milk in old-fashioned glass bottles. You pay a small deposit on the glass bottles, which you then get back when returning the bottle. The family-owned farm also offers their milk non-homogenized, which is incredibly fresh and wonderfully tasty. Their milk can also be purchased at several local farmers markets, independently owned grocery stores, or at their own farm. In addition to the creamy milk, they offer cream, butter, eggs, yogurt, and honey. Smyth's Trinity Farm also offers home delivery of their products to the five surrounding towns.

+ **TULMEADOW FARM** in West Simsbury, Connecticut, dates back to 1768 and originally started as a dairy farm. With rising costs, the farm no longer milks cows but rather raises grass-fed beef cattle instead. Don Tuller and his wife continue the farming tradition and offer packed steaks, ground beef, and pre-made hamburger patties in their farm store, along with offers of a CSA program for customers. The farm also grows many seasonal vegetables, which are sold in its busy farm store along with a wonderful selection of New England made goodies. In 1994, they decided to add making ice cream to their talents, with a goal to provide ice cream that would have guests coming back again and again. They now make more than 50 gourmet flavors of rich super-premium (16 percent butterfat) ice cream in pint and quart containers. Get a scoop of their famous ice cream at their farm store from April through October. One of my favorite flavors is the Black Raspberry with Chocolate Chunks (see page 63)—but eat your way through the selections and find your own preference. We sit on the hay bales overlooking the farm while devouring our creamy ice cream.

✦ **GOATBOY SOAPS** in New Milford, Connecticut, was prompted when one their children suffered from severe allergies and was only able to tolerate goat's milk. They began to raise a few goats, happened upon goat milk soap, and loved it. Lisa Agee and her husband Rick realized that most goat milk soap was made with powdered milk plus preservatives instead of the real thing. They decided to make their own all-natural goat milk soaps, resulting in the creamy GoatBoy Soaps that lather up with a ton of suds. Their amazing array of soaps are stacked up neatly in hefty natural wooden trays at many retail locations and local fairs throughout New England. Also be on the lookout for one of their incredible hand and body lotions, lip balms, and all-natural bug spray. I use Lisa's body lotion all year long, which helps keep my eczema under control and moisturized.

✦ **CROWLEY CHEESE** in Mount Holly, Vermont, has been creating award-winning cheeses using the same recipe since 1824. Hand-making cheese the old-fashioned way, with no additives or preservatives, the company uses fresh raw milk and unpasteurized milk to make all of their creamy cheeses. When the company was founded in the 1800s, there was obviously no refrigeration to store dairy. So the surrounding dairy farmers would bring their surplus milk to be made into cheese. Today, Crowley cheeses are made using the same methods and traditions first developed by the company's founder, Winfield Crowley. Their cheeses require patience and attention that only direct human involvement can create.

✦ **MAPLE MEADOW FARM,** located in Salisbury, Vermont, has been producing quality eggs since 1946 from their ultra-clean farmhouses of 65,000 laying hens. Their hens consist of Rhode Island Reds, which produce brown eggs, and White Leghorn hybrids, which produce white eggs. Sometimes their hens lay super jumbo eggs, which have two yolks and are too big to put into packaging. They have recently added a state-of-the-art facility to house 6,000 cage-free hens. They have a small retail store on their farm where you can buy their farm-fresh eggs and maple syrup as well as Monument Farm Dairy products. Their eggs are also available at many small independent grocery stores and local specialty stores.

✦ **TAYLOR FARM** in Londonderry, Vermont, has a quaint red barn farm stand where you'll find their farm-made cheeses and maple syrup. There are also locally made preserves, applesauce, and other confections. Their herd consists of 50 milking Holstein and Jersey cows, which all enjoy a free-stall barn. You'll feel right at home at their adorable farm and country store.

✦ **COOK FARM,** located in Hadley, Massachusetts, produces milk that it is pasteurized and bottled locally, so you know it's very fresh. They also make a wide variety of farm-made ice cream flavors and sell farm-fresh eggs, butter, cottage cheese, and cheddar cheeses. In operation since 1909, Cook Farm offers seasonal vegetables and fruits, along with locally produced maple syrup.

✦ **WRIGHT'S DAIRY FARM**, situated in North Smithfield, Rhode Island, is a family-run dairy farm serving the community for over 100 years. They offer customers the freshest, tastiest milk around because the milk never leaves the farm. There is also a retail store and bakery on the farm that is home to the most scrumptious baked goods like Danishes, coffee rolls, muffins, and scones along with custom cakes. Pick up farm-fresh eggs and local cheeses from other nearby farms at their store as well.

✦ **MAPLELINE FARM** in Hadley, Massachusetts, is a fifth-generation farm. In 2001, they decided to step back in time and offer home delivery of cream products and milk in glass bottles. For their home delivery, an insulated metal box on the porch keeps milk fresh in the heat or cold. Leave empty bottles in the porch box for them to pick up to sanitize and reuse. If you are in the area, stop by their farm to pick up your fresh milk.

✦ **NEIGHBORLY FARMS OF VERMONT** in Randolph Center, prides themselves on having a farm in tip-top shape, so it's pleasing to those who visit. They process wonderful certified organic farm-made cheeses by using pure and natural techniques, keeping the cows healthy and happy and ensuring that all the dairy products are wholesome and chemical free. Their cows are fed grains that have no antibiotics, and no commercial fertilizers are used on the farm. Stop by to see cows being milked and how they make the tastiest natural cheese.

✦ **SUGARBUSH FARM**, nestled in the hills of Woodstock, Vermont, specializes in making 14 cheese varieties the old-fashioned way. Selections include rich and creamy classic cheddar cheeses, plus specialty cheeses like hickory, maple-smoked, or horseradish cheddar. After sampling their award-winning cheese, walk on the nature trails and see the various farm animals. Visit the farm during sugaring season to watch and learn more about how maple syrup is made. Visit them year-round or soak up the colors of fall during leaf-peeping season.

✦ **GRAFTON CHEESE AND COUNTRY STORE** in Brattleboro, Vermont, near the banks of the winding river, is a wonderfully spacious country store stocked with a fabulous selection of Vermont-made products like pure maple syrup, locally produced honey, wine, farm-made jams, and all kinds of specialty foods. This state-of-the-art facility even has a second floor to view cheese-making. Stop by with the kids and check out the petting zoo.

FARMHOUSE BANANA BREAD

This banana bread recipe straight from the New England kitchen on our farm will melt in your mouth. It's moist and perfect with a freshly brewed cup of coffee. Try it hot out of the oven with farm-fresh butter.

Makes 3 loaves

1 CUP SHORTENING

1 TEASPOON PURE VANILLA EXTRACT

2 CUPS FIRMLY PACKED BROWN SUGAR

1/2 CUP GRANULATED SUGAR

3 LARGE EGGS

3 RIPE BANANAS, MASHED

1 1/2 CUPS FULL-FAT SOUR CREAM OR PLAIN WHOLE MILK YOGURT

3 1/2 CUPS ALL-PURPOSE FLOUR

1/2 TEASPOON KOSHER SALT

1 1/2 TEASPOONS BAKING POWDER

1 1/2 TEASPOONS BAKING SODA

1/2 CUP CHOPPED WALNUTS (OPTIONAL)

Preheat the oven to 350 degrees F. Line three 9 x 5-inch bread loaf pans with paper liners and set aside. (This makes cleanup very easy.)

In a large bowl, use a hand mixer to cream together the shortening, vanilla, and sugars. Add the eggs one at a time, beating well to incorporate. Add the bananas and sour cream to the mixture and thoroughly combine. Add the flour, salt, baking powder, and baking soda, stirring to combine. Add nuts and stir to combine. Divide the batter evenly into bread pans. Bake for 50 to 60 minutes, or until a toothpick inserted in the center comes out clean. Be very cautious not to move the pans abruptly while baking, as this will make the bread fall. Allow to cool on a baking rack.

FARMHOUSE PEANUT BUTTER COOKIES

Chocolate and peanut butter lovers beware! This yummy combination of peanut butter and chocolate will melt in your mouth, and it's sure to be become your favorite go-to cookie recipe. Note that when a cookie recipe calls for butter, never substitute with margarine; margarine tends to make cookies spread more. Maple sugar, which is used throughout the book, is a dry form of maple syrup that won't add extra moisture to the recipe. You can find it locally at sugarhouses, specialty food stores, or online.

Makes 3 dozen cookies

1 CUP (2 STICKS) BUTTER, SOFTENED

1 CUP GRANULATED SUGAR, PLUS MORE FOR DUSTING COOKIES

1 CUP FIRMLY PACKED BROWN SUGAR

1/2 CUP GRANULATED MAPLE SUGAR

1 CUP CREAMY PEANUT BUTTER

2 LARGE EGGS

1 TEASPOON PURE VANILLA EXTRACT

2 1/2 CUPS ALL-PURPOSE FLOUR

1/2 TEASPOON KOSHER SALT

1 1/2 TEASPOONS BAKING SODA

1 TEASPOON BAKING POWDER

1 CUP SEMISWEET CHOCOLATE CHIPS

Preheat the oven to 375 degrees F. Line baking sheets with parchment paper and set aside.

In a large bowl, use a hand mixer to cream together the butter, sugars, and peanut butter until light and fluffy. Beat in the eggs one at a time and add the vanilla.

In a medium bowl, combine flour, salt, baking soda, and baking powder. Add the dry ingredients to the wet mixture and stir to combine; mix in the chocolate chips. Shape dough into 1-inch balls and place on baking sheets.

Place a small amount of granulated sugar into a small, shallow bowl. Wet a fork and place it into the sugar; press the back of the fork into each ball of dough in two directions to make a crisscross pattern. Bake for 9 to 11 minutes, or until lightly golden brown. Remove cookies from the oven and cool on a baking rack.

LEMON ZEST CAKE

Since one of my favorite flavors is lemon, when I was a young girl, my mom would make a lemon pound cake in a Bundt cake pan and drizzle it with a simple lemon glaze. It's refreshing and flavorful. Top the cake with fresh sliced strawberries for a delicious twist.

Serves 6 to 8

FOR THE CAKE:

3 CUPS ALL-PURPOSE FLOUR

1 TEASPOON KOSHER SALT

3 TEASPOONS BAKING POWDER

$1/2$ CUP SHORTENING

$1/2$ CUP (1 STICK) UNSALTED BUTTER, SOFTENED

JUICE OF 1 LARGE LEMON

$2^1/2$ TEASPOONS PURE LEMON OIL

1 TEASPOON PURE VANILLA EXTRACT

$1^1/2$ CUPS GRANULATED SUGAR

3 LARGE EGGS

1 CUP WHOLE MILK

1 CUP FULL-FAT SOUR CREAM

FOR THE GLAZE:

$1^1/2$ CUPS CONFECTIONERS' SUGAR

1–2 TABLESPOONS FRESHLY SQUEEZED LEMON JUICE

2 TABLESPOONS SHORTENING

Preheat the oven to 350 degrees F. Prepare a Bundt pan by coating with cooking spray and a dusting of flour; set aside.

In a medium bowl, combine the flour, salt, and baking powder; set aside. In a large bowl, use a hand mixer on medium to high speed to cream together the shortening, butter, lemon juice, lemon oil, vanilla, sugar, and eggs. Use a spatula to scrape down the sides of the mixing bowl. To the lemon mixture, add half of the flour mixture, $1/2$ cup milk, and $1/2$ cup sour cream. Mix on low to combine, then add the remaining flour mixture, $1/2$ cup milk, and $1/2$ cup sour cream. Again, mix on low to thoroughly combine.

Pour the cake batter into the pan, and make sure cake better is level. Bake for 35 to 40 minutes, or until a toothpick inserted into the cake comes out clean. Remove the cake from the oven and allow to sit for 5 minutes in the pan on a cooling rack. Flip the cake onto the cooling rack and remove the pan. Allow to cool completely.

To make the glaze, combine confectioners' sugar, lemon juice, and shortening in a medium bowl; whisk thoroughly. Pour the glaze over the cake and serve.

CHOCOLATE-PEANUT BUTTER WHOOPIE PIES

Whoopie pies are a staple in Maine and other New England states. This particular recipe was inspired by our summer vacations at Acres of Wildlife, where they have a bakery in their country store that makes all sorts of goodies.

Makes 1 dozen

FOR THE CHOCOLATE WHOOPIE PIE:

1/2 CUP VEGETABLE SHORTENING

1/2 CUP GRANULATED SUGAR

1/2 CUP FIRMLY PACKED BROWN SUGAR

2 LARGE EGGS

2 1/2 CUPS ALL-PURPOSE FLOUR

1 TEASPOON KOSHER SALT

1 TEASPOON BAKING POWDER

1/2 TEASPOON BAKING SODA

3/4 CUP HIGH-QUALITY, UNSWEETENED COCOA POWDER

1 CUP WHOLE MILK

1/2 CUP FULL-FAT VANILLA GREEK YOGURT

1 TEASPOON PURE VANILLA EXTRACT

FOR THE PEANUT BUTTER FROSTING:

1/2 CUP VEGETABLE SHORTENING

2 OUNCES FULL-FAT CREAM CHEESE, SOFTENED

1/2 CUP CREAMY PEANUT BUTTER

2 CUPS CONFECTIONERS' SUGAR

1/4 TEASPOON KOSHER SALT

2 TABLESPOONS WHOLE MILK

Preheat the oven to 350 degrees F. Line a baking sheet with parchment paper and set aside.

In a large bowl, use a hand mixer to cream together shortening and sugars. Add the eggs one at a time, and mix to combine.

Sift together the flour, salt, baking powder, baking soda, and cocoa powder. Alternately add the dry ingredients, milk, and yogurt into the shortening mixture, stirring to make sure they are fully incorporated and scraping the bowl with a spatula as needed. Add the vanilla extract and combine.

Using two tablespoons, scoop spoonfuls of batter onto the baking sheet, making round mounds of batter and aiming for 24 cake mounds. Be sure to leave space between the mounds, as the batter will spread a little. Bake for 15 to 16 minutes; turn the baking sheet once, halfway through the baking process. Remove cakes from baking sheet and allow to cool completely on cooling racks.

To make the frosting, in the bowl of a stand mixer cream together the shortening, cream cheese, peanut butter, and confectioners' sugar. Add the salt and milk, and continue to beat until whipped and creamy. Spread peanut butter frosting on the flat side of a cooled cake and sandwich together with another cake.

RED VELVET WHOOPIE PIES

This whoopie pie is super moist and finger-licking delicious. I use a cream cheese frosting for the filling. Put the frosting into a plastic bag and cut off a small corner to easily pipe it onto the cake creations.

Makes 1 dozen

FOR THE WHOOPIE PIES:

½ CUP VEGETABLE SHORTENING

1 CUP GRANULATED SUGAR

½ CUP FIRMLY PACKED BROWN SUGAR

2 LARGE EGGS

1 CUP FULL-FAT GREEK YOGURT

½ CUP COCOA POWDER

2 TEASPOONS PURE VANILLA EXTRACT

1 OUNCE RED FOOD COLORING

2½ CUPS ALL-PURPOSE FLOUR

1 TEASPOON KOSHER SALT

1 TEASPOON BAKING SODA

1 TABLESPOON APPLE CIDER VINEGAR

FOR THE CREAM CHEESE FROSTING:

¾ CUP VEGETABLE SHORTENING

4 OUNCES FULL-FAT CREAM CHEESE, SOFTENED

4 CUPS CONFECTIONERS' SUGAR

1 TEASPOON KOSHER SALT

1 TEASPOON PURE VANILLA EXTRACT

3 TABLESPOONS WHOLE MILK

Preheat the oven to 350 degrees F. Line a baking sheet with parchment paper and set aside.

In a large mixing bowl, cream together the shortening, sugar, and brown sugar. Add one egg at a time and combine. Scrape the bowl with a rubber spatula. Add the Greek yogurt, cocoa, and vanilla; combine. Add the food coloring and mix in well. Add the flour and salt. In a separate bowl, combine the baking soda and vinegar. Gently stir into the batter.

Using two tablespoons, scoop spoonfuls of batter onto the baking sheet, making round mounds of batter and aiming for 24 cake mounds. Be sure to leave space between the mounds, as the batter will spread a little. Bake for 16 to 18 minutes, turning the baking sheet once, halfway through the baking process. Remove cakes from baking sheet and allow to cool completely on cooling racks.

To make the frosting, in the bowl of a stand mixer cream together the shortening, cream cheese, and confectioners' sugar. Add the salt, vanilla, and milk, continuing to beat until whipped and creamy. Spread cream cheese frosting on the flat side of a cooled cake and sandwich together with another cake.

RASPBERRY-CHOCOLATE CHUNK ICE CREAM

Inspired by one of my absolute favorite ice cream flavors at Tulmeadow Farm in West Simsbury, Connecticut.

Makes 1 pint

3 CUPS FRESH RASPBERRIES

1/2 CUP WATER

2 CUPS HEAVY CREAM

1 1/2 CUPS WHOLE MILK

1/2 TEASPOON KOSHER SALT

2 LARGE EGG YOLKS

1 CUP GRANULATED SUGAR

1/2 TEASPOON PURE VANILLA EXTRACT

1/2 TEASPOON FRESHLY SQUEEZED LEMON JUICE

1 1/2 CUPS SEMISWEET CHOCOLATE CHUNKS

In a large saucepan, add the raspberries and water and cook over low to medium heat for about 10 minutes. Press the raspberry puree through a fine-mesh strainer into a bowl. Put the raspberry juice back into the saucepan and discard the pulp and seeds. Add the cream, milk, and salt; whisk to combine. Bring the mixture just to a simmer over medium heat, stirring with a wooden spoon. Remove from heat and allow to sit for 30 minutes.

In a medium bowl whisk together the egg yolks and sugar for about 2 minutes. Gradually whisk in 1/2 cup of the warm cream mixture. Transfer the yolk mixture into the remaining cream mixture in the saucepan, whisking to combine. Cook mixture over medium heat, stirring constantly, until thick enough to coat a wooden spoon, 2 to 3 minutes. Stir in vanilla extract and lemon juice. Using a rubber spatula, scrape custard into a medium bowl and set over a bowl of ice; allow to cool, stirring occasionally. Process custard in an ice cream maker according to manufacturer's instructions. Add the chocolate chunks at the end of the ice cream cycle. Transfer to an airtight container and freeze until firm.

RUSTIC APPLE SPICE BREAD

This recipe comes from the kitchen of my father's dear friend Edward Bendza. I was fortunate enough to be given all of his perfected recipes and discovered that his Rustic Apple Spice Bread is a wonderful treat for breakfast or an afternoon dessert. Use whatever apples are in season. I find that Macoun apples are a fabulous variety that pack a wallop of flavor and bake well.

Makes 2 loaves

3 CUPS ALL-PURPOSE FLOUR

3 TEASPOONS BAKING POWDER

1/2 TEASPOON BAKING SODA

1 1/2 TEASPOONS KOSHER SALT

1 CUP FIRMLY PACKED BROWN SUGAR

1 1/2 CUPS OLD-FASHIONED ROLLED OATS

2 TEASPOONS GROUND CINNAMON

1/2 TEASPOON GROUND NUTMEG

2 1/4 CUPS GRATED APPLES

1/2 CUP CHOPPED WALNUTS

1/2 CUP RAISINS (OPTIONAL)

3 LARGE EGGS

1/2 CUP WHOLE MILK

1/4 CUP FULL-FAT SOUR CREAM

1/2 CUP VEGETABLE OIL

Preheat the oven to 350 degrees F. Line two 9 x 5-inch bread loaf pans with paper liners.

In a large mixing bowl, use a spoon or spatula to combine the flour, baking powder, baking soda, salt, brown sugar, oats, cinnamon, and nutmeg. Add the apples, nuts, raisins, eggs, milk, sour cream, and oil; combine thoroughly. Divide the batter evenly into the prepared pans and bake for 60 to 65 minutes, or until a toothpick inserted into the center comes out clean. Be very cautious not to move the pans abruptly while baking, as this will cause the bread to fall. Let cool on a baking rack and enjoy.

CREAMY CHEDDAR AND BROCCOLI SOUP

This soup is wonderful on a cold, snowy winter day with the aroma filling your kitchen. I love to add crushed crackers to the soup when it's served or to serve the soup in a sourdough bread bowl.

Serves 6 to 8

¼ CUP (½ STICK) UNSALTED BUTTER

1 POUND BACON, CUT INTO 1-INCH PIECES

1 CUP CHOPPED PORTOBELLO MUSHROOMS

2 MEDIUM ONIONS, MEDIUM DICE

1 POUND BROCCOLI, MEDIUM DICE

SALT AND FRESHLY GROUND BLACK PEPPER

¼ CUP FINELY CHOPPED FRESH CHIVES

1 TABLESPOON ITALIAN SEASONING

2–3 TABLESPOONS WHITE WINE

4 CUPS CHICKEN STOCK

2 CUPS WHOLE MILK

2 CUPS HEAVY CREAM

½ CUP ALL-PURPOSE FLOUR

10 OUNCES SHREDDED SHARP CHEDDAR CHEESE

In a large Dutch oven, melt butter over medium-high heat. Add the bacon, mushrooms, and onions. Sauté until onion is softened and bacon is browned, stirring occasionally. Add the broccoli, and season to taste with salt and pepper; stir. Add chives, Italian seasoning, white wine, and stock, using a wooden spoon to scrape brown bits up from the bottom of the pan as you add ingredients. Bring to a boil and simmer until broccoli is tender, 10 to 15 minutes.

In a measuring cup, whisk together the milk, heavy cream, and flour until the flour is dissolved; pour into soup, stirring frequently until thickened. Reduce the heat and stir in the cheese until melted. Serve.

NEW ENGLAND CLAM CHOWDER

Nothing could be fresher than seafood from the coast of Maine. There's nothing quite like a hot cup of clam chowder on a moonlit summer's night overlooking the ocean. Crumble some buttery oyster crackers over top and enjoy.

Serves 6 to 8

6 SLICES BACON, CUT INTO SMALL PIECES

1 LARGE ONION, DICED

½ CUP (1 STICK) UNSALTED BUTTER

¼ CUP ALL-PURPOSE FLOUR

2 CUPS WATER

1 CUP CLAM JUICE

2 MEDIUM OR LARGE RUSSET POTATOES, PEELED AND CUT INTO ½-INCH CUBES

2 CUPS HALF-AND-HALF

½ TEASPOON KOSHER SALT

3 (6.5-OUNCE) CANS MINCED CLAMS WITH JUICE

1 TABLESPOON DRIED PARSLEY

½ CUP WHOLE MILK

FRESHLY GROUND BLACK PEPPER

In a 2-quart saucepan on low to medium heat, cook the bacon until browned. Add the onion; cook until onion is slightly transparent. Add the butter and melt, then add the flour to the saucepan and stir briskly. The mixture will start to thicken. Add the water, clam juice, and potatoes. Cook until the potatoes are soft, 20 to 30 minutes. Gradually add the half-and-half to the pan while stirring briskly. The mixture will be creamy and thick. Add the salt, clams, parsley, and milk; add pepper to taste. Turn the heat down to low and simmer gently for about 15 minutes, stirring frequently.

MAINE LOBSTER STEW

The rocky coast of Maine is filled with gorgeous views, mountainsides covered in purple and blue lupine flowers, and wildlife in salt marshes. Utilizing the state's incredible fresh seafood, this recipe is from the rural kitchen of my husband's stepmother's grandmother.

Serves 6 to 8

3 TABLESPOONS UNSALTED BUTTER

1 LARGE ONION, SLICED

1 CUP DICED FRESH LOBSTER MEAT

JUICE FROM LOBSTER MEAT (IF USING FRESH LOBSTERS)

1 TEASPOON KOSHER SALT

1/8 TEASPOON PAPRIKA

4 CUPS WHOLE MILK OR 2 CUPS WHOLE MILK AND 2 CUPS LIGHT CREAM

2 TABLESPOONS CHOPPED PARSLEY, FOR GARNISH

In a large pot, melt the butter over medium-high heat. Sauté the onion in butter until it is soft and translucent. Add lobster, lobster juice, salt, and paprika. Cook on low heat. Add the milk and bring to a simmer, using caution not to scorch the milk. Simmer for 10 minutes. Taste, and adjust seasonings, if necessary. Garnish with parsley and serve.

HOMEMADE

ARTISANAL BREADS, STICKY BUNS & CONFECTIONS

Bread baking runs in my family. When I was growing up, my mom had a growing bread list: she would take orders each week, and my dad would deliver the loaves to neighbors and co-workers every Thursday. She loved to bake and used this as a little income for our household, while also obsessing about perfecting all her bread and pizza dough recipes.

There are many incredible bakeries throughout New England that achieve awesome results by using simple and natural ingredients for recipes. Also, there are a number of gourmet food manufacturers still handcrafting products from recipes that have been handed down from generation to generation. Many of these wonderful bakeries offer café-style shops where you can sip hot coffee and savor their sweet pastries or even nibble on a sandwich while enjoying a conversation with a close friend. Stop in at your local bakery for some freshly baked artisan bread that has a crunchy and chewy crust just bursting with flavors. Countless bakeries in New England are family-owned and operated, offering a personal atmosphere.

We love to bake at home. It's a wonderful way to get children involved in the kitchen, spend time together as a family, and learn about measurements. Our children have fun helping measure flour, crack eggs, and overall, learning how to bake. Nothing tastes better than apple pie with a flaky crust paired with homemade vanilla ice cream, especially when your kids have had a hand in making them. In addition, baking at home helps you control where your food comes from and what ingredients go into it. Wholesome grains and fresh dairy, berries, and eggs will make your baked goods ooze with deliciousness.

Baking bread at home might seem like a challenging task, but it's extremely rewarding. When I bake bread, I set a good duration of time to allow for the bread to rise properly and bake perfectly. Since I am already baking, making a few extra loaves to freeze is no problem. Also, making pizza at home is super easy and saves money. Top the pizza with ingredients already in the fridge. For those times you might not have time to bake, there are plenty of fabulous New England bakeries to choose from.

✦ **SEVEN STARS BAKERY** in Providence, Rhode Island, was opened in 2001 by Lynn and Jim Williams with a goal to bake great breads and treats that customers would love. The bakery features a splendid café where you can sip trade-free and organic coffee while enjoying a warm cinnamon bun drizzled with icing. Also be sure to try one of their melt-in-your-mouth croissants. Breads are handmade with organic ingredients along with old-fashioned methods of long, slow fermentation to develop a unique flavor and texture. Everything is baked daily using fresh butter, local eggs, and organic grains and flours. They have two locations in Providence and one recently opened location in Rumford, Rhode Island.

✦ **GRAY'S GRIST MILL**, situated on the Massachusetts and Rhode Island border in Westport, Massachusetts, is a historical treasure dating back to the early 1700s. Grist mills were commonplace in New England during earlier times with mills being built to grind grains into usable meals. Early settlers relied on grist mills to provide flour and cornmeal for baking. They were built near the water because they needed the water for electricity. Often other businesses, such as sawmills, blacksmith shops, and general stores, were built in the surrounding area. Gray's Grist Mill is still in operation and produces a unique Johnny Cake meal and several pancake mixes.

✦ **CLEAR FLOUR BREAD BAKERY** in Brookline, Massachusetts, specializes in making authentic breads of Italy and France as well as incredible from-scratch pastries. They use fresh, simple ingredients with flours that are unbleached, have no preservatives, and are organic and stone-ground. No additives of any kind are added to anything they bake. Enjoy scrumptious handmade donuts filled with fresh raspberry preserves and sprinkled with powdered sugar along with freshly brewed coffee. My personal favorite is probably one of their delightful cream puffs.

✦ **FLOUR BAKERY & CAFÉ** in Boston, Massachusetts, makes mouthwatering pastries that are bursting with lemon curd, raspberry preserves, and fresh made-to-order salads and sandwiches. Their use of fresh, natural ingredients and inventive recipes make for scrumptious cookies and crusty breads. In a warm and inviting atmosphere, sit and sip hot, sinfully delicious coffee from an oversized mug. Afterwards, stroll down the picturesque streets of Boston and absorb some of America's great history. The architecture is simply breathtaking in this seaside town full of row houses and vintage buildings.

✦ **A & J KING ARTISAN BAKERS** in Salem, Massachusetts, makes artisan breads using time-honored traditions. Artisan breads take a great deal of time and effort to make, so their products should be enjoyed with great pleasure. No preservatives or unnatural ingredients are used in any of their breads or pastries. Baking with good, wholesome, natural ingredients, they use local berries in their freshly baked pastries. They are open year-round and offer many seasonal specials.

✦ **SWEET DREAMS BAKERY** in Stratham, New Hampshire, is a family-run bakery steeped in tradition. Stop by daily to pick up freshly baked breads, chocolate éclairs, peanut butter cookies, and rich brownies. For lunch or dinner you can have a tasty sandwich made on one of their freshly baked breads—my favorite being the honey-baked ham on oatmeal molasses bread.

✦ **BROWN HOUSE BAKERY** in Harrisville, New Hampshire, is located in the historic mill town and offers a wide variety of artisan-baked goods. Visit them in New Hampshire or have their wonderful creations shipped right to your home. They are known for their amazing coffee cakes and other wonderful sweet creations, including almond-raspberry thumbprint cookies, pecan bars, and granola trail mix.

✦ **RED HEN BAKING COMPANY** in Middlesex, Vermont, offers premium-quality breads and pastries with traditional methods. Owners Randy George and Liza Cain strive for minimal negative impact on the environment, as both producers and consumers. They believe that good food is one of life's great pleasures, and that it's worth great time and effort to make delicious food that nourishes both the body and spirit. They insist on using incredibly fresh and organic ingredients.

✦ **LITTLETON GRIST MILL** dates back to 1797 and is located in Littleton, New Hampshire. While the mill has changed ownership several times throughout the years, it has now been completely restored by private funds. It is open to the public as a working museum, and it is still grinding organically grown grains for flour and pancake mixes, cereals, and granolas that are sold in specialty shops throughout the Northeast.

✦ **KENYON'S GRIST MILL** in West Kingston, Rhode Island, is the oldest operating manufacturing business in Rhode Island. Their current building dates back to 1886, but the mill has been grinding meals and flours since 1696. They work closely with local bakeries and farm stands to produce all-natural rye flour and breads. They purchase as much locally grown grains as possible, never sourcing grains with additives, pesticides, or preservatives. The grist mill produces cornmeal and many different flours and mixes, including clam cake mix, cornbread mix, and old-fashioned pancake mixes.

✦ **SONO BAKING COMPANY AND CAFÉ** in South Norwalk, Connecticut, is a bakery to enjoy not just coffee and a pastry, but also a freshly made panini. With an open kitchen and bakery, you can view artisan breads being pulled from the oven, pastries being filled with fresh preserves, and cakes being frosted. The café offers a simple and delicious menu within an inviting setting. SoNo isn't the only café you should visit while walking down the streets in South Norwalk. Stop by **CHOCOPOLOGIE**, one of the finest European-style cafés. Eat a light lunch or delicious dinner while watching them handcraft incredible chocolates and pastries.

✦ **MYSTIC MARKET EAST** is an adorable deli and bakery sitting right in the heart of the quaint seaside town of Mystic, Connecticut. It is a wonderful place to grab a freshly made sandwich for lunch or a tasty pastry that was baked early that morning. Their lovely store also offers an array of locally made gourmet foods, sauces, honeys, and soup mixes. Grab your lunch and stroll the streets of Mystic where the smell of salt water touches your nose. While you're there, visit Mystic Seaport to wander into the depths of maritime history.

✦ **LA PETITE FRANCE** in West Hartford, Connecticut, is a warm and inviting bakery that was started by Paris transplants now residing in Connecticut. Their bakery offers authentic French breads (that are crunchy on the outside and chewy on the inside), croissants, and pastries. Also offered are pumpernickel, sourdough, rye, and whole wheat breads, all made fresh daily; pastries vary depending on what is in season. From June through mid-October, they are also available at several farmers markets. It's a wonderful opportunity to pick up your fresh baked goods and support local businesses.

✦ **HARVEST BAKERY** in Bristol, Connecticut, now in its fourth generation of operation, has an incredible selection of the most tempting old-fashioned pastries, donuts, cookies, and breads. Martin Hurwitz and his wife, Jackie, still use original recipes from the 1940s and hearth-bake all of their breads. Their scrumptious baked goods and crunchy artisan breads will delight any food connoisseur. Warm breads come right out of the oven just waiting to be enjoyed with fresh homemade beef stew. You can special order cakes, pastries, and bread bowls for any occasion.

✦ **STONEWALL KITCHEN** in York, Maine, was started when Jonathan King and his partner, Jim Scott, sold jars of jam at the local farmers market. Now, they have grown to be the manufacturers of wonderful mustards, condiments, jams, and baking mixes—some of my personal favorites are their Maple Balsamic Dressing, Wild Maine Blueberry Jam, and Roadhouse Steak Sauce. Tour their facility to see jams, sauces, and other sinfully delicious specialty foods being created. Afterward, stop by their store for all sorts of fabulous kitchen gadgets, cutting boards, dish towels, and specialty foods. Their store is bright with exposed beams and gorgeous hardwood floors; the spacious farmhouse kitchen tables boast glass jars filled with gourmet cookies, spatulas, wooden rolling pins, farmhouse ceramic bowls, baking trays, and colorful cupcake baking cups. After you've shopped, eat lunch in their café or sit on their stone patio and absorb the beauty of their carefully manicured gardens.

✦ **KING ARTHUR FLOUR** in Norwich, Vermont, offers baking classes and freshly baked pastries, cookies, and breads. They also offer ingredients and baking mixes that let you do your very best baking. The store is packed full of wonderful kitchen gadgets, baking sheets, pots and pans, and more. At various times of the year, you can bring your kids to decorate their own mini gingerbread house, watch chefs create recipes in their demo kitchen, and enjoy product samples.

When you are looking for the very best kitchen gadgets made in New England, you can't go wrong with **VERMONT ROLLING PINS**. They handcraft each and every one of their rolling pins out of maple, cherry, or walnut wood. Great for rolling out pizza dough or pastry crust, gorgeous handmade rolling pins are the perfect addition to any kitchen. Each rolling pin is crafted by an artisan who works the wood with a lathe to obtain the desired shape. Afterwards, the rolling pin is sanded to a smooth finish and oiled to enhance the natural wood grain and color. They offer a wide array of choices for everyone's taste.

HOMEMADE PIZZA DOUGH

At my house we love making homemade pizza. Use tomato sauce, a 4-cheese pizza blend (which melts nicely), and any desired toppings. Or, for a unique twist, layer the pizza with grilled chicken pieces, caramelized onions, and Gorgonzola cheese. You can make your own garlic-infused olive oil or purchase it—I like a company called Garlic Heads.

Makes 4 to 6 pizzas (10 to 12 inches each)

1 TABLESPOON DRY ACTIVE YEAST

1¼ CUPS WATER, WARM (115 DEGREES F)

2 TABLESPOONS HONEY

2 TABLESPOONS GARLIC-INFUSED OLIVE OIL

1 TEASPOON KOSHER SALT

4½–5 CUPS ALL-PURPOSE OR BREAD FLOUR

OLIVE OIL

CORNMEAL

DESIRED PIZZA TOPPINGS

In the bowl of a stand mixer, add the dry yeast to the warm water and stir. Add the honey and olive oil and stir. Add the salt and 3 cups flour; attach the dough hook to the stand mixer and combine mixture. Gradually add more flour until the dough pulls away from the sides of the bowl. Turn the dough out onto a lightly floured surface and knead until smooth, 4 to 5 minutes. Lightly coat the mixing bowl with a little bit of olive oil, and return the dough, smooth side up, to the bowl. Cover loosely with plastic wrap and let rise in a warm place for about 2 hours.

Place a pizza stone inside the oven and preheat to 550 degrees F. Turn dough out onto a lightly floured surface and cut into 4 to 6 pieces, depending on how small you want your pizzas. Shape the pieces into rounds and roll out the dough you are going to immediately use on a lightly floured surface; place the rest in a freezer bag. Unused dough can be kept in the fridge for up to 1 week or in the freezer for up to 1 month.

Sprinkle about 1 teaspoon cornmeal onto a wooden pizza paddle. Drizzle the dough with about 1 tablespoon olive oil, and spread it over the surface with the back of a spoon. Add desired toppings and transfer pizza to pizza stone. Gently slide the pizza quickly back and forth to make sure it doesn't stick to the paddle while transferring. Cook for 8 to 10 minutes, or until the cheese is bubbly and golden brown. Remove from oven using the pizza paddle.

MAPLE SHREDDED WHEAT BREAD

Here's another recipe from Bendza, who was a kind and spirited man. He was the type of person who told you exactly how it was, and I always admired that honesty. He developed and perfected dozens of bread recipes, but this one is my personal favorite.

Makes 2 loaves

4 LARGE SHREDDED WHEAT BISCUITS, CRUMBLED

2¾ CUPS BOILING WATER

¼ CUP VEGETABLE OIL

½ CUP MAPLE SYRUP

½ CUP FIRMLY PACKED BROWN SUGAR

2¾ TEASPOONS KOSHER SALT

1½ TABLESPOONS ACTIVE DRY YEAST

⅓ CUP WATER, WARM (105–115 DEGREES F)

6½ CUPS ALL-PURPOSE FLOUR

¼ CUP WHEAT GERM

In a large bowl, cover the shredded wheat with boiling water. Add the oil, syrup, brown sugar, and salt. Stir. Let mixture cool to a lukewarm temperature.

In a small bowl, dissolve the yeast in warm water. Add the dissolved yeast, flour, and wheat germ to the shredded wheat mixture to create firm dough. Knead by hand on a lightly floured surface until smooth. Spray a medium bowl with cooking spray, return dough to the bowl, and cover loosely with plastic wrap. Let dough rise until doubled in size, 1 to 1½ hours.

Grease 2 (9 x 5-inch) loaf pans and set aside.

Turn dough out onto a lightly floured surface and knead for 8 to 10 minutes. Shape into 2 loaves and place into loaf pans. Cover loosely with plastic wrap and let rise until doubled, 1 to 1½ hours.

Preheat the oven to 375 degrees F. Bake for approximately 40 minutes, or until golden. Remove bread from pans and allow to cool on a cooling rack.

FARMHOUSE CINNAMON RAISIN BREAD

This bread is sure to remind you of your grandmother's baking. Its old-fashioned style will leave you wanting it every day for breakfast, toasted with your favorite homemade jam. In our household, it usually doesn't make it to the next day. We cut right into it while it's still warm.

Makes 2 loaves

1 CUP WHOLE MILK

¾ CUP WATER

½ CUP BROWN SUGAR

1½ TABLESPOONS ACTIVE DRY YEAST

3 CUPS ALL-PURPOSE FLOUR

2½–3 CUPS WHOLE WHEAT FLOUR

2 TEASPOONS KOSHER SALT

1 LARGE EGG

¼ CUP VEGETABLE OIL

1 CUP RAISINS

½ CUP GRANULATED MAPLE SUGAR

½ CUP GRANULATED SUGAR

1 TABLESPOON CINNAMON

2 TABLESPOONS BUTTER, MELTED

In a medium saucepan, heat the milk, water, and brown sugar until just warm. Remove from heat and dissolve the yeast in the heated milk mixture.

In a large bowl, combine the all-purpose and wheat flours and salt. Starting with $2^{1}/_{2}$ cups of flour mix, add to milk mixture. Using a hand mixer, beat for about 3 minutes to combine thoroughly. Gently stir in the egg, oil, and raisins. Add the remaining flour to make a moderately soft dough. Turn the dough out onto a lightly floured surface and knead for 8 to 10 minutes. Spray the mixing bowl with cooking spray and return the dough to the bowl. Cover with plastic wrap and allow to rise for about $1^{1}/_{2}$ hours, or until doubled.

Spray 2 (9 x 5-inch) loaf pans with cooking spray and set aside.

In a small bowl, combine the maple sugar, granulated sugar, and cinnamon; set aside.

Divide the dough in half and place on a lightly floured surface. Using a rolling pin, roll each portion into a rectangle shape. Brush each section of dough with $^{1}/_{2}$ tablespoon melted butter and sprinkle with cinnamon-sugar mixture. Beginning at the narrow end, roll up the dough, tightly pressing dough into the roll at each turn. Press ends to seal and fold ends under loaf. Place dough into pans. Brush with remaining melted butter, cover loosely with plastic wrap, and let rise until doubled, about 45 minutes.

Preheat the oven to 375 degrees F.

Bake for 35 to 40 minutes, until golden. Remove from oven and allow to cool for 5 minutes on a cooling rack. Remove from bread pans and cool.

GRANDMA LAMOTHE'S CREAM PUFFS

Every year for the holidays and special occasions, my French-Canadian grandmother always took time to make real homemade goodness for everyone, including these cream puffs. So much thought and effort went into everything she made, along with so much love. While she cooked, she told stories about growing up during the Great Depression, coming from Canada at a young age, and the hardships their family went through.

Serves 8

FOR THE CREAM PUFFS:

1 CUP WATER

½ CUP VEGETABLE SHORTENING

¼ TEASPOON KOSHER SALT

1 CUP ALL-PURPOSE FLOUR

4 LARGE EGGS

FOR THE CREAM FILLING:

1 (3.4-OUNCE) PACKAGE VANILLA INSTANT PUDDING

1 CUP WHOLE MILK

1 TEASPOON ALMOND EXTRACT

1 PINT HEAVY CREAM

FOR THE CHOCOLATE GLAZE:

¾ CUP SEMI-SWEET CHOCOLATE CHIPS

1 TABLESPOON BUTTER

2 TEASPOONS HEAVY CREAM

2 TEASPOONS CORN SYRUP

MARASCHINO CHERRIES, MINT LEAF CANDIES, AND CONFECTIONERS' SUGAR, FOR GARNISH

To make the cream puffs, in a medium saucepan bring the water to a boil. Add the shortening and salt. Let the water return to a full boil and then remove from heat. Add the flour, stirring until the mixture forms a ball and leaves the sides of the pan. Using a hand mixer on high speed, add the eggs one at a time, making sure to mix well between additions. The mixture will be very smooth and silky looking. Allow cream puff batter to cool.

Meanwhile, preheat the oven to 425 degrees F and line a baking sheet with parchment paper.

Using two large tablespoons, drop the batter in about 9 scoops on the sheet in a circle. Bake for 15 minutes; reduce oven temperature to 350 degrees F and bake for an additional 30 minutes. Remove from oven and set pan on a rack to cool.

To make the cream filling, in a large bowl add the vanilla pudding, milk, and almond extract; blend together. Cover with plastic wrap and set aside in the refrigerator. When ready to fill the cream puffs, add the heavy cream to a large bowl and use a hand mixer to whip to soft peaks. Fold the pudding mixture and whipped cream together using a spatula. Slice the tops off of the cream puffs, removing and discarding some of the pastry with your fingers. Scoop the filling into each cream puff.

To make the chocolate glaze, create a double boiler by bringing a medium pot of water to a boil over medium heat. Place a heatproof bowl on top of the boiling water, adding the chocolate chips, butter, heavy cream, and corn syrup to the bowl. Stir mixture together with spatula until chocolate is melted and combined. Drizzle warm chocolate over the top of the cream puffs. Decorate with drained maraschino cherries and mint leaf candies. Sprinkle with confectioners' sugar.

GREAT-GRANDMA EUNICE KUZY'S MOLASSES COOKIES

Every time my mother bakes these cookies, she tells the story of when she was a kid, her mother once made these and forgot to indent the cookies with fork marks. My mother's brother refused to eat them because they couldn't be grandma's cookies without those marks. This recipe is a staple during holiday time.

Makes 3 dozen cookies

1 CUP FIRMLY PACKED BROWN SUGAR

1 CUP MOLASSES

1¼ CUPS UNSALTED BUTTER, SOFTENED

1 LARGE EGG, BEATEN

1 TEASPOON APPLE CIDER VINEGAR

2 TEASPOONS BAKING SODA

1 TEASPOON KOSHER SALT

1½ TEASPOONS GROUND CINNAMON

1 TEASPOON GROUND NUTMEG

2 TEASPOONS GROUND GINGER

½ TEASPOON GROUND CLOVES

5 CUPS ALL-PURPOSE FLOUR

¾ CUP SUGAR

In a large mixing bowl cream together the brown sugar, molasses, and softened butter. Add the egg and gently combine ingredients together. Add the vinegar, baking soda, salt, cinnamon, nutmeg, ginger, cloves, and flour, mixing to combine ingredients. Transfer dough to a plastic bag; refrigerate for 1 to 2 hours.

Preheat the oven to 375 degrees F. Line several half sheet pans with parchment paper and set aside.

Remove chilled dough from refrigerator and roll cookie dough into 2-inch rounds. Roll rounds in granulated sugar and place on a baking sheet, leaving a bit of space for them to spread. Use a fork to make cross marks. Bake cookies until lightly browned, 12 to 14 minutes.

CHOCOLATE-DIPPED SHORTBREAD COOKIES

I've always been the type of mom who makes everything from scratch. Each holiday, I create something handmade for teachers, the postman, bus driver, and anyone else needing a little special gift. These yummy shortbread cookies are great for a simple yet extremely flavorful homemade treat.

Makes 18 to 24 cookies

1 CUP (2 STICKS) BUTTER, SOFTENED

½ CUP GRANULATED SUGAR

½ CUP CONFECTIONERS' SUGAR

½ TEASPOON PURE VANILLA EXTRACT

½ TEASPOON PURE LEMON EXTRACT

1 LARGE EGG

3 CUPS ALL-PURPOSE FLOUR

1 TEASPOON KOSHER

1–2 CUPS SEMISWEET CHOCOLATE CHIPS

TOASTED COCONUT, SLICED ALMONDS, OR SPRINKLES FOR GARNISH (OPTIONAL)

In a large bowl, use a hand mixer to cream together the butter, sugars, and extracts. Add the egg and mix together. In a medium bowl, sift together flour and salt. Gradually add the flour into the butter mixture, mixing well. Scrape the sides of the bowl with a spatula to make sure all of the ingredients are thoroughly combined. Flatten the dough into a disc shape and place in a plastic bag. Refrigerate for at least 30 minutes.

Meanwhile, preheat the oven to 350 degrees F, and line 2 baking sheets with parchment paper.

Using a rolling pin, roll out the dough on a lightly floured surface to an approximately ¼-thick round. Use a cookie cutter to cut out cookies in desired shape, and place cookies on the baking sheets. (If the dough becomes too soft to work with, return it to the refrigerator for a few minutes.) Bake until lightly browned, 8 to 10 minutes. Transfer cookies to a wire cooling rack and let cool.

Line a baking sheet with parchment paper and set aside. Place chocolate in a double boiler and stir with spatula until it is melted. Dip one end of each shortbread cookie into melted chocolate and place on the baking sheet. Before the chocolate dries, you can sprinkle with sliced almonds, toasted coconut, or colored sprinkles. Keep the shortbread cookies in an airtight container, or wrap them individually in cellophane bags to give as gifts.

MAPLE-APPLE OAT MUFFINS

Apples make these muffins extra moist, and with the combination of winter spices, these make a wholesome addition to any breakfast or afternoon tea.

Makes 18

FOR THE MUFFINS:

2 LARGE EGGS

½ CUP (1 STICK) UNSALTED BUTTER, SOFTENED

1 CUP MAPLE SYRUP

1½ CUPS DICED APPLES

2 CUPS ALL-PURPOSE FLOUR

1 CUP OLD-FASHIONED ROLLED OATS

1 TABLESPOON BAKING POWDER

1 TEASPOON KOSHER SALT

1 TEASPOON GROUND CINNAMON

1 TEASPOON GROUND NUTMEG

FOR THE TOPPING:

2 TABLESPOONS BROWN SUGAR

1 TABLESPOON ALL-PURPOSE FLOUR

1 TABLESPOON BUTTER, SOFTENED

¼ TEASPOON GROUND CINNAMON

Preheat the oven to 350 degrees F. Prepare 2 muffin pans with paper liners.

In a large bowl, use a hand mixer to cream together the eggs and butter until light and fluffy. Add the maple syrup and apples, mixing well to combine.

In a medium bowl, add the flour, oats, baking powder, salt, cinnamon, and nutmeg; stir to combine. Incorporate the dry ingredients into the butter mixture, stirring to combine. Pour batter into prepared muffin tins.

In a small bowl, combine all the topping ingredients. Sprinkle the topping on the muffins. Bake for 20 to 25 minutes, until muffins are light golden and a toothpick inserted in the center comes out clean.

MAPLE-CINNAMON GRANOLA

Homemade granola is the perfect addition to yogurt, making it a hearty snack that is whole-some and simple to make.

Makes 3 pounds

2 POUNDS ROLLED OATS

1 CUP RAW HULLED SUNFLOWER SEEDS

2 CUPS RAISINS

2 CUPS PECANS

1 TEASPOON GROUND CINNAMON

3 TABLESPOONS WATER

1/2 TEASPOON KOSHER SALT

1 CUP MAPLE SYRUP

1/2 CUP HONEY

1/2 CUP VEGETABLE OIL

1 TEASPOON PURE VANILLA EXTRACT

Preheat the oven to 300 degrees F. Lightly grease 2 (9 x 12-inch) baking pans and set aside.

In a large bowl, mix together the oats, sunflower seeds, raisins, pecans, and cinnamon. In a small pot, bring the water to a boil over high heat, and stir in salt to dissolve. Then stir in the maple syrup, honey, and oil, and bring mixture to a simmer. Remove from the heat, and whisk in the vanilla. Immediately pour maple syrup mixture over the oat mixture. Stir completely so the oat mixture is evenly coated. Divide evenly between the 2 pans and bake for 30 minutes. Store in an airtight container for up to 3 weeks.

BLUEBERRY COFFEE CAKE WITH STREUSEL TOPPING

What better way to enjoy your cake and berries together than with this scrumptious dessert? This cake combines two of Maine's treasured harvests—maple syrup and blueberries. Travel to Maine from July to September to find wild Maine blueberries at nearly every roadside stand. Buy more than you need and freeze for later use.

Serves 6 to 8

FOR THE CAKE:

2 CUPS ALL-PURPOSE FLOUR

1 CUP MAPLE SYRUP

1 TEASPOON BAKING POWDER

1 TEASPOON KOSHER SALT

½ CUP (1 STICK) UNSALTED BUTTER, SOFTENED

1 CUP WHOLE MILK

2 LARGE EGGS

1 CUP FRESH BLUEBERRIES

FOR THE STREUSEL TOPPING:

½ CUP CHOPPED PECANS

½ CUP FIRMLY PACKED BROWN SUGAR

¼ CUP GRANULATED MAPLE SUGAR

FOR THE GLAZE:

2 CUPS CONFECTIONERS' SUGAR

1 TEASPOON PURE VANILLA EXTRACT

1 TABLESPOON FRESHLY SQUEEZED LEMON JUICE

Preheat the oven to 350 degrees F. Grease a 9 x 13-inch baking pan and set aside.

To make the cake, in a large bowl combine all ingredients together except blueberries. Using a hand mixer, mix on medium speed for 2 minutes, scraping bowl occasionally with a spatula. Spread half the batter in the pan. Sprinkle the blueberries over the batter, and then top with the remaining batter.

In a medium bowl, mix together streusel topping ingredients. Top batter with streusel topping.

Bake until the top is golden and a toothpick inserted in the center comes out clean, approximately 40 minutes. Allow to cool slightly before adding glaze.

In a medium bowl, mix together confectioners' sugar, vanilla, and lemon juice until desired consistency. Drizzle glaze over cake and serve.

LEMON RUM CAKE

My mother worked very hard to make this luscious cake perfectly moist with just the right balance of lemon and rum. This cake is wonderful any time of year and is quick to prepare. Growing up in our house, you always needed dessert. My father insisted upon it.

Serves 6 to 8

FOR THE CAKE:

¾ CUP (1 ½ STICKS) UNSALTED BUTTER

1 ½ CUPS GRANULATED SUGAR

3 LARGE EGGS

1 TABLESPOON PURE LEMON EXTRACT

⅜ TEASPOON KOSHER SALT

3 CUPS ALL-PURPOSE FLOUR

1 TABLESPOON BAKING POWDER

¾ CUP WHOLE MILK

FOR THE SYRUP:

1 ½ CUPS FRESHLY SQUEEZED LEMON JUICE

1 CUP GRANULATED SUGAR

¼ CUP RUM

FOR THE BERRY TOPPING:

1 PINT FRESH RASPBERRIES

2 TABLESPOONS GRANULATED SUGAR

Preheat the oven to 350 degrees F. Generously grease a 12-cup fluted tube pan and set aside.

In a large bowl, use a hand mixer to cream together the butter and sugar. Add the eggs and beat well. Add the lemon extract. In a medium bowl, sift together the salt, flour, and baking powder. Add the dry ingredients, alternating with the milk, into the butter mixture, mixing on low speed to combine. Pour batter into the prepared pan. Bake until a toothpick comes out clean when inserted into the cake, 40 to 50 minutes.

Meanwhile, prepare the syrup. In a microwave-safe bowl, add the lemon juice and sugar. Microwave for about 2 minutes, or until sugar is dissolved. Add the rum, stir to combine, and set aside.

In a medium bowl, combine the raspberries and sugar; allow to stand for 30 minutes to 1 hour to bring out the natural juices.

When the cake has cooled in the pan for about 5 minutes, remove from cake pan and let cool completely on a wire rack. Place the cake back in the pan and poke holes with a large fork. Pour the syrup over the cake. Let the cake sit in the pan to absorb the syrup for about 10 minutes. Remove from the pan and place on a serving plate. Top with raspberries.

BLUEBERRY MUFFINS

Our son Mason loves farm-fresh blueberries; I usually have to buy one pint just for him to eat whenever I make a blueberry recipe, like these all-time favorite muffins.

Makes 12 muffins

1 CUP ALL-PURPOSE FLOUR

½ TEASPOON KOSHER SALT

½ TEASPOON BAKING SODA

1 TEASPOON BAKING POWDER

5 TABLESPOONS UNSALTED BUTTER, MELTED

½ CUP FIRMLY PACKED BROWN SUGAR

2 LARGE EGGS

1 TEASPOON PURE VANILLA EXTRACT

1 CUP OLD-FASHIONED ROLLED OATS

½ CUP MAPLE SYRUP

1 CUP FRESH OR FROZEN BLUEBERRIES

Preheat the oven to 375 degrees F. Line a muffin pan with 12 paper liners and set aside.

In a medium bowl, combine the flour, salt, baking soda, and baking powder; mix well. In a large mixing bowl, cream together the melted butter and brown sugar, add eggs one at a time, and add vanilla; blend. Add the rolled oats and maple syrup to the egg mixture and combine. Mix in the dry ingredients. Stir only until blended (mixture will be lumpy). Fold in the blueberries. Scoop the batter into the muffin cups. Bake for 25 to 30 minutes, or until golden brown. Allow to cool, and then remove from the pan.

PIONEER BREAD

This recipe is from my father's good friend Edward Bendza, who would join us at the farm every Tuesday, Thursday, and Saturday morning for coffee break without fail. He was especially talented in the garden and at raising laying hens. He was also a perfectionist in the kitchen with a love for baking bread and developed numerous recipes using organic ingredients.

Makes 2 loaves

½ CUP YELLOW CORNMEAL

⅓ CUP FIRMLY PACKED BROWN SUGAR

⅓ CUP MAPLE SYRUP

2 TEASPOONS KOSHER SALT

¼ CUP VEGETABLE OIL

1 CUP BOILING WATER

3 TEASPOONS DRY YEAST

⅓ CUP LUKEWARM WATER (105–115 DEGREES F)

1 CUP COOL WATER

½ CUP WHEAT GERM

½ CUP WHOLE WHEAT FLOUR

½ CUP RYE FLOUR

2–2½ CUPS ALL-PURPOSE OR BREAD FLOUR

In a large mixing bowl, combine the cornmeal, brown sugar, maple syrup, salt, and oil with the boiling water. In a small bowl, dissolve the yeast in lukewarm water. Add the cool water and dissolved yeast to the cornmeal mixture. Add the wheat germ, wheat flour, and rye flour. Stir to combine and stir in enough all-purpose flour make a firm dough. Turn dough out onto a lightly floured surface and knead until smooth. Spray the mixing bowl with cooking spray and return the dough to the bowl. Cover loosely with plastic wrap and allow dough to rise until doubled in size, about 1 hour.

Meanwhile, grease 2 (9 x 5-inch) loaf pans and set aside.

After dough has risen, divide in half. Knead each piece of dough on a lightly floured surface for 8 to 10 minutes. Shape into 2 loaves and place into the pans. Cover lightly with plastic wrap and let rise for about 1 to 1½ hours.

Preheat the oven to 375 degrees F.

Bake bread for 35 to 40 minutes, until golden. Carefully remove bread from each pan and allow to cool on a cooling rack.

TAPPING THE SOURCE
A NEW ENGLAND TRADITION
OF SUGARING

My family began making maple syrup before I could even walk. My dad tapped all the neighborhood trees, and we collected the sap each afternoon when he got home from work. The snow was so deep that it was a quite a task to walk with heavy buckets filled with sap. At that point, we used only galvanized buckets and taps. To collect the sap, my dad would get plastic five-gallon buckets from the local bakery, and we would carry two buckets each. We walked from tree to tree collecting all the sap and then back to the truck to dump it in the tank.

The early spring months are what New Englanders call the "fifth season," or mud season, when maple sap starts flowing in the trees. The days are longer and the weather is warming up. During the night, the temperature still dips below freezing. At a sugarhouse, the burrows of steam escape from the open cupola doors and the smell of sweet sugar is in the air.

Galvanized buckets hanging off sugar maple trees are a sure sign that maple season or "sugaring season" is upon us. Maple syrup is a labor of love with an intensive process of tapping sugar maple trees, gathering the sap daily, and boiling it down to a sweet, tasty reward. Maple sap is perishable, thus requiring it to be collected and boiled down daily. It is a lot of work to complete in a season that lasts only about 6 to 8 weeks. Sugar makers spend many sleepless nights boiling sap into the wee hours of dawn. It takes approximately 43 gallons of sap to make just 1 gallon of maple syrup. Maple syrup is sometimes referred to as "liquid gold" since it takes so much time to make and is expensive, but very much worth every penny! (Also note that there are different grades of maple syrup. The darker the syrup, the stronger and richer it tastes. Syrup labeled "very dark" is fantastic in recipes and has the most intense maple flavor.)

Legend has it that Native Americans were the first to discover maple syrup, or as they called it, "sinzibukwud." It is said that they made V-shaped incisions in the trees and let the sap drip into a hollowed-out piece of birch wood below. They didn't have proper storage for maple syrup, so most of their syrup was made into hard bricks of maple sugar. Maple sugar enabled them to travel with it, and keep it for longer periods of time. Later, settlers would introduce wooden buckets and iron and copper kettles as well as drills, augers, and wooden spouts (or spiles) to aid in streamlining the process. Native Americans showed French settlers how to tap trees at the outset of spring, harvest the sap, and boil it to evaporate the water. Maple syrup production was important at this time because other types of sugar were expensive and hard to find.

Today, there are an abundance of sugarhouses to visit all over New England. Some sugarhouses in New Hampshire, Massachusetts, Maine, and Vermont even serve full breakfasts during the peak of the season. With all the different sugarhouses, you'll find some still using old-time traditions of boiling sap with a wood-fired evaporator and others who have converted to more modern practices. The Department of Agriculture in each state usually will provide a list of area sugarhouses to visit, which includes whether they are open to the public, hours of operation, and if they offer a retail store.

✦ **MAPLE CORNER FARM** in Granville, Massachusetts is a sugarhouse now in its eighth generation of farming and producing maple syrup with a large wood-fired evaporator in a rustic, old-fashioned sugarhouse. From late February to early April, enjoy a tasty breakfast at their pancake restaurant. They also offer cross-country skiing and snow shoeing, with a wide variety of trails for different experience levels. Warm up near the fireplace, or enjoy a warm bowl of chili or soup while resting your tired feet. They also produce hay and offer pick-your-own blueberries, in addition to selling maple syrup, maple products, and homemade jams and jellies year-round. Tours are also offered during sugaring season.

✦ **NORTH HADLEY SUGAR SHACK** in Hadley, Massachusetts, serves New England pancake breakfasts along with their pure maple syrup. They are open Wednesday through Sunday, starting in mid-February through mid-April. Their restaurant uses their own farm-grown strawberries and buys blueberries and eggs from local farms. The dairy and cream products used at their restaurant are from Mapleline Farm in Massachusetts. They reopen in mid-August and are open daily until December 23, offering pumpkins, Indian corn, gourds, straw, and mums. During the holiday season, maple gift baskets, wreaths, and Christmas trees are available for purchase.

✦ **BASCOM FAMILY FARMS** in Alstead, New Hampshire, has its sugarhouse high on top of the mountain overlooking the valley on 2,200 acres. Making syrup since 1853, they are now the largest producer of maple syrup in New England. In its seventh generation of family-run farming, they offer an incredible inventory of maple syrup–making supplies. Bascom's also buys and sells maple syrup in bulk.

✦ **POLLY'S PANCAKE PARLOR** in New Hampshire is set close on a winding road that offers impeccable views of picturesque Sugar Hill. Staring out as a seasonal restaurant only open during sugaring season, this cute pancake parlor is now open daily for a fresh taste of New England. Pancakes are made from scratch every day from wholesome ingredients. Alongside the pancakes, they serve smoked bacon, sausage patties, and smoked ham that are all made locally at North Country Smokehouse. Their pancake parlor is in the original 1830 building, which has been updated over the years. Their eggs are fresh and the coffee is ground daily. The aromas of smoked bacon on the griddle and freshly prepared pancakes will tempt your every taste bud.

✦ **RED BUCKET SUGAR SHACK** in Worthington, Massachusetts, is open February through early April. You can watch maple syrup being made on their wood-fired evaporator and enjoy breakfast in their rustic dining room. The smells of warm maple syrup and sweet creamy butter fill the air of the restaurant. Their specialty pancakes will impress even the most persnickety customer. There's also a cute gift shop in the sugarhouse, where you can purchase real maple syrup, maple candies, and other novelties.

✦ **GOULD'S MAPLE SUGARHOUSE** in Shelburne, Massachusetts, has a very charming rustic appeal. The gray gravel driveway brings you to a deep rust red color sugarhouse, which houses a wood-fired evaporator. Steam billows out of the cupola doors on top of the sugarhouse that has been producing maple syrup for six generations. Stop by their sugarhouse for many wonderful maple confections and breakfast during sugaring season.

✦ **EATON'S SUGARHOUSE** in South Royalton, Vermont, is a fun place to visit. Enjoy the sweet treasures of a New England tradition by watching maple sap boil or maple candy and maple cream being made. Stop by their restaurant and enjoy a wonderful breakfast featuring freshly made waffles drizzled in 100 percent pure maple syrup. They also serve good old-fashioned dinners in addition to their delightful breakfasts. Their country store offers a wide variety of unique gourmet foods, old-style toys, jams, maple syrup, and creamy cheeses.

✦ **MORSE FARM MAPLE SUGARWORKS** in Montpelier, Vermont, is one of the oldest farms in the state, now in its eighth generation of producing maple syrup. Still using a wood-fired evaporator, Morse Farm currently has over 3,000 taps. The sweet smell of maple sap being boiled down to syrup fills the air during March and into early April. Burr Morse and his family make everything from pure maple candies and kettle corn to fudge, maple cream, and other confections. Their farm store is abundant with all sorts of wonderful handmade maple products and Vermont-made goodies.

✦ **BRAGG FARM SUGARHOUSE** in East Montpelier, Vermont, has also been producing quality maple syrup for eight generations. Doug Bragg and his family still work hard on this farm to collect maple sap and create handmade maple products for families to enjoy. They are still making maple syrup the old-fashioned way using galvanized buckets (over 2,500 of them) to collect sap and boiling it over wood-fired evaporators.

✦ **LAMOTHE'S SUGAR HOUSE** in Burlington, Connecticut, offers a wide variety of maple products, including tasty maple barbeque sauce, maple kettle corn, and maple dip. A dark rust-color Golden Retriever will happily greet arrivals to the farm. Their country gift store with hardwood floors, lots of natural light, and rustic wooden hutches is filled with syrup, honey, and farm-made jams. The store boasts handmade offerings like locally grown eggs, fresh cheeses, and other flavorful New England–based gourmet foods. Family run and operated, they started in the early 1970s with only a few taps and quickly have become one of the largest sugarhouses in Connecticut, now with over 5,500 taps. They look for innovative ways to produce maple syrup while helping the environment. They are open year-round, with maple syrup–making demonstrations on the weekends during February and March.

✦ **STUART & JOHN'S SUGAR HOUSE** in Westmoreland, New Hampshire, is owned and operated by two friends who started tapping maple trees in 1974 with about 920 taps. With help from their families, the sugarhouse has grown in size and now has approximately 10,000 taps. Tour their sugarhouse and watch maple syrup being made February through early April. They have a restaurant as well, which is open on the weekends in the autumn and February through April during sugaring season. During the summer months, the restaurant is open daily as an ice cream parlor, featuring hot fudge maple sundaes and many other yummy treats. You'll also find a delectable selection of seafood, burgers, salads, and wraps at the restaurant during the summer.

CARING FOR MAPLE SYRUP

As long as the original container of maple syrup is unopened and kept in a cool, dry place, it can be kept almost indefinitely. Once you open a container of maple syrup, it needs to be refrigerated. Maple syrup and granulated maple sugar can be used anywhere you would use white or brown sugar, such as to sweeten coffee and tea or as a sugar substitute in any recipe. Should your syrup at any time develop mold, simply pour it into a saucepan, bring it to a boil over high heat, and skim off the mold. It will then be ready to use again.

MAPLE SYRUP GRADES

- Grade A pure maple syrup for retail sale is available in four color classes:

- Golden has a light to golden color with a delicate or mild taste.

- Amber has a light amber color and a rich or full-bodied taste.

- Dark has a dark color and a more robust taste than the lighter color classes.

- Very Dark is very dark in color and offers a strong taste; it is recommended for cooking, but some consumers prefer it for table use.

HOW TO TAP A SUGAR MAPLE TREE

Tap only sugar maple trees, which are identified by their bark. The bark on young trees is dark gray. On mature trees, the bark is dark brown and has developed vertical grooves and ridges. The edges of the plates gradually lift as a sugar maple gets older, and the plates flake away from top to bottom once the tree has reached ample maturity. In the fall, their leaves turn brilliant colors of orange, red, and amber. Swamp maples have jagged edges on the leaves. They can be tapped, but it takes 80 gallons of sap to produce 1 gallon of syrup—not a great ratio. The leaf of a sugar maple is rounded at the base, extending to generally 5 lobes without fine teeth.

Select only healthy trees. Sometimes trees near the roadside are not healthy because of exposure to road salt. A tree must be 16 inches in diameter to tap with 1 tap, over 21 inches for 2 taps, and 27 inches in diameter for 3 taps.

Don't over-tap the trees—use your judgment on adding more taps. Distribute multiple taps equally around the circumference of the tree. Use a $^7/_{16}$ drill bit ($^5/_{16}$ for health spouts) angled slightly upward to help facilitate sap flow. Drill the hole 2 to $2^1/_2$ inches in depth and 12 inches up or down from the current hole. It needs to be several inches side to side from previous tap holes. There must be no dark-colored wood, which indicates dead wood, when you drill the new hole. If you do hit dead wood, simply drill a new hole farther away. Lightly tap in the spout with a hammer, hang the bucket, and use the lid to keep out any debris, rainwater, snow, etc.

Temperatures must be freezing or below at night and above 40 degrees F during the day. Once trees bud, the syrup season is over; syrup collected after that will have an awful "buddy" taste. Pull taps after the season ends. The tree will naturally heal the area. Wash all equipment with soapy water; rinse well and let air dry. Do not use bleach!

BUREAU'S SUGARHOUSE PANCAKE AND WAFFLES

This is an old-school pancake and waffle batter but worth the effort. Don Bureau and his family have been perfecting this yummy recipe for the last 30 years. I'm sure you will enjoy it as much we did.

3 LARGE EGGS

2 CUPS ALL-PURPOSE FLOUR

3 TABLESPOONS GRANULATED MAPLE SUGAR

3 TEASPOONS BAKING POWDER

¼ TEASPOON KOSHER SALT

¼ CUP CANOLA OIL

2 CUPS BUTTERMILK, PLUS MORE IF NEEDED

2 TEASPOONS PURE VANILLA EXTRACT

BLUEBERRIES (OPTIONAL)

CHOCOLATE CHIPS (OPTIONAL)

APPLE CHUNKS (OPTIONAL)

BUTTER, MELTED (OPTIONAL)

Separate the egg yolks from the whites and divide into individual bowls.

In a large bowl, combine the flour, maple sugar, baking powder, and salt. Add the egg yolks, oil, buttermilk, and vanilla extract. Whisk by hand until the mixture is very smooth. Add a little more buttermilk if the batter is too thick.

In a medium bowl, beat egg whites until stiff peaks form. With a spatula, fold the egg whites into the batter. Be careful not to deflate the egg whites.

For pancakes, spoon the batter onto an oiled cast-iron pan on low-to-medium heat. Drop in fresh blueberries, chocolate chips or chunks of apples. Cook until lightly golden and then flip over to cook the other side. Top with pure maple syrup.

For waffles, cook on a waffle iron. Do not add fruit to the batter, as it will stick. Top with melted butter, fresh fruit, and pure maple syrup.

MAPLE FRENCH TOAST

In our house, Sunday is a day to just relax and enjoy each other's company. Our lives are so busy that it has become very important to reconnect with each other and take one day each week to unwind. During the spring and summer, after a delicious breakfast of French toast, we usually help my parents sell product at the local farmers market. Of course, maple has always been a fixture in our lives, and we really enjoy its goodness.

Makes 12 to 14 pieces

6 LARGE EGGS

½ CUP WHOLE MILK

½ CUP HEAVY CREAM

1 TEASPOON PURE VANILLA EXTRACT

1 TEASPOON GROUND CINNAMON

½ TEASPOON GROUND NUTMEG

½ TEASPOON KOSHER SALT

1 LOAF DAY-OLD ITALIAN BREAD, CUT INTO 1-INCH SLICES, OR TEXAS TOAST BREAD

1 TABLESPOON BUTTER, PLUS ADDITIONAL FOR SERVING

MAPLE SYRUP, FOR SERVING

CONFECTIONERS' SUGAR, FOR SERVING

In a large bowl, combine the eggs, milk, and heavy cream and whisk together. Add the vanilla, cinnamon, nutmeg, and salt, stirring to combine.

Dip each bread slice one at a time into the mixture. Melt the butter in a large nonstick skillet over medium heat, and add as many pieces of bread as will fit in the skillet. Cook each side for about 3 minutes, or until golden brown. Serve with butter, warm maple syrup, and a sprinkle of confectioners' sugar.

MAPLE-CINNAMON BUNS

These ooey-gooey treats are pure heaven. Making treats like this from scratch takes time, but they are worth the effort. Your taste buds will thank you.

Makes about 15 buns

FOR THE BUNS:

4 CUPS ALL-PURPOSE FLOUR

1/3 CUP GRANULATED SUGAR

1 TEASPOON KOSHER SALT

2 (.25-OUNCE) PACKAGES ACTIVE DRY YEAST (4 1/2 TEASPOONS)

1 CUP MILK, VERY WARM

1/4 CUP (1/2 STICK) BUTTER, SOFTENED

1 LARGE EGG

FOR THE FILLING:

1 CUP FIRMLY PACKED BROWN SUGAR

3/4 CUP GRANULATED MAPLE SUGAR

1 TEASPOON GROUND CINNAMON

1/4 TEASPOON GROUND CLOVES

1/2 TEASPOON GROUND NUTMEG

2 TABLESPOONS UNSALTED BUTTER, SOFTENED

1/2 CUP CHOPPED PECANS (OPTIONAL)

FOR THE ICING:

2 CUPS CONFECTIONERS' SUGAR

1 TEASPOON PURE VANILLA EXTRACT

1/2 CUP MASCARPONE CHEESE OR SOFTENED CREAM CHEESE

2–3 TEASPOONS WHOLE MILK

In a large bowl, mix together 2 cups flour, sugar, salt, and yeast. With a hand mixer, add the warm milk, butter, and egg. Beat on low speed until mixed. Use a spatula to scrape down the sides of the bowl. Stir in the remaining 2 cups flour. Place dough on a lightly floured surface. Knead for about 5 minutes, until smooth. Spray a large bowl with cooking spray. Place dough in bowl, cover loosely with plastic wrap, and set the bowl in warm place. Let rise for about 1 1/2 hours, or until doubled.

To make the filling, combine the brown sugar, maple sugar, cinnamon, cloves, nutmeg, and butter in a small mixing bowl.

Transfer the dough to a lightly floured surface, and use a rolling pin to roll the dough into a rectangle. Spread 1/4 cup butter over surface of the dough, and sprinkle filling evenly over the top. Sprinkle nuts over the filling. Beginning with the longer side, roll the dough tightly. Pinch together to seal, and cut into 1-inch slices with a sharp serrated knife.

Preheat the oven to 350 degrees F. Line a 9 x 13-inch baking pan with parchment paper and coat with cooking spray. Place cinnamon buns into the pan, leaving some space between them. Let rise in a warm place until doubled, about 30 minutes. Bake until lightly golden brown, about 30 minutes. Allow the buns to cool.

To make the icing, add sugar, vanilla, and mascarpone cheese into a medium bowl. Stir, adding milk a little bit at a time until desired consistency is achieved. Drizzle over the cooled buns and serve.

MAPLE CREAM SPREAD

Dip fruit into this delicious spread or use it to top bagels, scones, and English muffins. It also works for a simple frosting glazed onto pound cake or homemade doughnuts.

Serves 4 to 6

8 OUNCES CREAM CHEESE, SOFTENED

½ CUP MAPLE SYRUP

½ CUP CHOPPED WALNUTS
(OPTIONAL)

In a small bowl, combine the cream cheese, maple syrup, and nuts. Refrigerate until ready to serve.

MAPLE BACON

Nothing is better than the sweet and salty taste of bacon coated with a touch of maple sugar. It's the perfect addition to any breakfast or even a burger off the grill.

Makes 1 pound bacon

1 POUND BACON

1 TABLESPOON GRANULATED MAPLE
SUGAR

Preheat the oven to 400 degrees F.

Line the bacon on a baking sheet. Sprinkle with the granulated maple sugar and bake until bacon is crispy, about 20 minutes.

MAPLE CHEESECAKE

Maple syrup has its own distinct flavor that makes this cheesecake stand above the rest in this twist on the classic. Top the cheesecake with fresh strawberries from the farmers market.

Serves 6 to 8

FOR THE CRUST:

2½ CUPS GRAHAM CRACKER CRUMBS

½ CUP GRANULATED SUGAR

⅔ CUP BUTTER, SOFTENED

FOR THE FILLING:

8 OUNCES CREAM CHEESE

¾ CUP MAPLE SYRUP

1 LARGE EGG

¾ CUP SOUR CREAM

¼ CUP HEAVY CREAM

1 TEASPOON PURE VANILLA EXTRACT

FRESH STRAWBERRY SLICES, FOR SERVING

Preheat the oven to 350 degrees F.

In a medium bowl, mix together the graham cracker crumbs, sugar, and butter to make the crust. Press the mixture into the bottom of a 9-inch springform pan and set aside.

In a large bowl, add the cream cheese, syrup, egg, sour cream, heavy cream, and vanilla; mix together thoroughly with a hand mixer. Pour into prepared springform pan. Bake for 1 hour. Turn oven off and leave the cheesecake inside for 2 hours, making sure not to open the oven at all during this time. Remove from the oven and refrigerate for about 1 hour. Run a knife around outside edge of the cheesecake to loosen from pan. Remove the side of the pan from the bottom, and serve cheesecake with strawberries.

MAPLE PEACH BARBEQUE SAUCE

I created this recipe in the commercial kitchen at my parent's sugarhouse. Its sweet yet tangy vibrancy pairs well with pork or chicken for a taste of summer. This sauce can also be combined with balsamic vinaigrette in a 1 to 1 ratio ($^1/_4$ cup barbeque sauce to $^1/_4$ cup balsamic vinaigrette) and poured over a juicy steak.

Makes about 3 cups

$^3/_4$ CUP CIDER VINEGAR

$^1/_2$ CUP TOMATO PASTE

1 CUP 1-INCH CUBES FRESH PEACHES

$^1/_2$ CUP MOLASSES

$^3/_4$ CUP MAPLE SYRUP

$^1/_2$ CUP WATER

1 TABLESPOON ONION POWDER

1 TEASPOON GARLIC POWDER

1 TABLESPOON FIRMLY PACKED BROWN SUGAR

1 TABLESPOON FRESHLY SQUEEZED LEMON JUICE

$^1/_2$ TEASPOON GROUND MUSTARD

$^1/_2$ TEASPOON FRESHLY GROUND BLACK PEPPER

$^1/_2$ TEASPOON KOSHER SALT

$^1/_2$ TEASPOON GROUND CAYENNE PEPPER

$^1/_2$ TEASPOON PAPRIKA

In a medium saucepan, add all the ingredients and cook over medium heat, whisking together to dissolve any lumps. Cook until the peaches are softened and the sauce has thickened to desired consistency, about 20 minutes. To check the thickness, transfer a small amount to a small cup, and place it in the freezer until cool.

MAPLE-APPLE COFFEE CAKE

Apples are a big part of New England's produce bounty. Adding maple syrup and sour cream make this particular cake wonderfully moist and flavorful.

Serves 6 to 8

FOR THE CAKE:

½ CUP (1 STICK) UNSALTED BUTTER, SOFTENED

1 CUP GRANULATED MAPLE SUGAR

2 LARGE EGGS

1 TEASPOON PURE VANILLA EXTRACT

1 TEASPOON BAKING SODA

1 TEASPOON BAKING POWDER

½ TEASPOON KOSHER SALT

2 CUPS ALL-PURPOSE FLOUR

1 CUP SOUR CREAM

2 TART APPLES, PEELED, CORED, AND CHOPPED

FOR THE TOPPING:

½ CUP BROWN SUGAR

2 TABLESPOONS UNSALTED BUTTER, SOFTENED

1 TEASPOON GROUND CINNAMON

½ TEASPOON GROUND NUTMEG

½ CUP CHOPPED WALNUTS (OPTIONAL)

FOR THE ICING:

2 CUPS POWDERED SUGAR

1 TEASPOON VANILLA EXTRACT

2 TEASPOONS WHOLE MILK

Preheat the oven to 375 degrees F. Grease and flour a Bundt pan and set aside.

In a large bowl, cream the butter and maple sugar using a hand mixer. Add the eggs and vanilla, mixing well to combine. In a medium bowl, mix together baking soda, baking powder, salt, and flour. Alternating with sour cream, add dry ingredients to butter mixture. Fold in the apples. Pour mixture into the Bundt pan.

In a medium bowl, combine the topping ingredients. Sprinkle topping over the batter. Bake for approximately 40 minutes. Test with a toothpick; if it comes out clean, the cake is done. Let the cake cool in the pan for 5 to 10 minutes. Remove from pan, allow to cool completely before drizzling with icing.

To make the icing, add sugar and vanilla into a medium bowl. Stir, adding milk a little bit at a time until desired consistency is achieved.

MAPLE-NUT FUDGE

This unusual take on basic fudge will wow everyone who tastes it.

Serves 6 to 8

2 CUPS GRANULATED SUGAR

1 CUP MAPLE SYRUP

2 TABLESPOONS CORN SYRUP

¾ CUP WHOLE MILK

1 TABLESPOON UNSALTED BUTTER

1 TEASPOON PURE VANILLA EXTRACT

1 CUP CHOPPED WALNUTS (OPTIONAL)

Prepare a bowl of ice water large enough to fit a large saucepan inside and set aside. Grease an 8 x 8-inch square baking pan and set aside.

In a large saucepan over medium heat, add the sugar, maple syrup, corn syrup, and milk. Stir continuously with a wooden spoon to completely melt the sugar. Allow the mixture to boil, letting it come to a soft ball stage, which is approximately 238 degrees F on a candy thermometer. Remove from heat and stir in the butter and vanilla. Set the saucepan in ice water. Do not touch it until mixture is luke-warm. Take the saucepan out of the water and stir until it is no longer shiny and loses the glossy look. Pour the fudge into the baking pan and sprinkle walnuts over the top. Cut into pieces when completely cooled and store in an airtight container in the refrigerator for up to 2 weeks.

THE LOCAL SPIRITS

WINERIES & VINEYARDS

New England offers a slice of the most amazing wineries and vineyards in the area. Some produce their own unique wines with distinct flavors and tastes. Because of the cooler New England climate, some produce berry wines, brandies, fruit wines, and ciders as well as wines. One of the keys to New England wine has been the development of cold-hardy grapes, which match well with the northern microclimates. Many of the New England states offer wine tours for premier vineyards and wineries. Some wineries even host farm-to-table dinners, concerts, and special tasting events during their harvest season. If you are a wine lover, drive through the lush countryside of New England and visit these independent, family-owned vineyards, and take home a few bottles to enjoy with your home-cooked dinners.

✦ **HOPKINS VINEYARD**, overlooking the hills of New Preston, Connecticut, is one of the area's best vineyards to sample wines and taste different cheeses. Family owned since 1787, the spectacular views look over the rolling hills of New England. The vineyard offers an array of unique wines produced in their state-of-the-art facility. Their spacious country store offers a wide variety of New England–made gourmet foods, kitchenware, and their own local honey.

✦ **JONATHAN EDWARDS WINERY** in North Stonington, Connecticut, crafts both Napa Valley, California, and Connecticut estate wines to capture tastes of both coasts' unique climates. When you go there, expect to stay and enjoy a good portion of your day beyond their beautiful tasting room. Feel free to bring a picnic lunch or cheese and crackers to enjoy while sipping the flavors of their wines on the patio overlooking the vineyard. As an added bonus, learn about the wine-making process, their vineyard, and what makes their wines unique. The winery is also a stunning venue for weddings and events.

✦ **SHARPE HILL WINERY** in Pomfret, Connecticut, not only produces amazing wine but also has one of the state's finest restaurants, the Fireside Tavern. The restaurant offers scrumptious gourmet lunches and dinner overlooking the beautiful perennial gardens and estate. The wine-tasting room is open year-round every Friday, Saturday, and Sunday. Pomfret is a quaint and charming town to visit beyond the winery, so plan accordingly.

✦ **CHARLOTTE VILLAGE WINERY** in Charlotte, Vermont, offers complimentary wine tastings from Memorial Day weekend through the first of January. The winery features both grape and fruit wines. Some of the wines offered are Strawberry Riesling, Raspberry, Peach Chardonnay, Merlot, and three different blueberry wines. The winery also features stunning views of the picturesque hills of Vermont.

✦ **SHELBURNE VINEYARD** sits high above the rolling hills of Shelburne, Vermont. This state-of-the-art winery is incredibly manicured, with a tasting room boasting large, sun-filled windows. The newly renovated earthy building is eco-friendly and energy-efficient. Inside you'll find gorgeous stone floors and a tasting bar crafted from locally harvested cherry wood. Their retail store is filled with all of their handcrafted wines, local gourmet foods, kitchen gadgets, crafts, and more.

✦ **FLAG HILL** is a beautiful winery set amongst the mountains in Lee, New Hampshire, and it's one of the largest in the area. They grow grapes that are able to adapt to the cooler climates of New England. The spacious tasting room features charming espresso-colored wood floors, wooden crates filled with wine, and kitchen accessories. They also have an executive chef and staff ready to assist for a special event or wedding.

✦ **GREENVALE VINEYARDS** in Portsmouth, Rhode Island, produces incredible-tasting estate-grown wines. The picturesque setting presents rows of grapes that produce approximately 3,500 cases of wine each year. The 5,000-square-foot tasting room has a very earthy and raw feel to it and sits inside a newly renovated 1863 historic stable.

✦ **BARTLETT MAINE ESTATE WINERY** in Gouldsboro, Maine, offers more than 20 varieties of wine, including Bartlett's Reserve Blueberry Wine, Pear-Apple White Wine, blackberry dessert wines, and honey meads, with an emphasis on quality, not quantity. Their tasting room, housed in a unique hand-wrought stone building, is open seasonally June through October or off-season by appointment.

✦ **SWEETGRASS FARM WINERY AND DISTILLERY** is situated in Union, Maine, and produces wonderful apple wines, cranberry gin, rum, and apple brandy. This family-run company is deeply rooted in the community and supports local sustainable agriculture. Hike trails, enjoy a picnic lunch, and catch your breath with sweet northern breezes.

✦ **BLACKSMITH'S WINERY**, located in South Casco, Maine, is full of rustic charm. The winery is open year-round and offers a wonderful selection of locally produced wines. The tasting room has a natural wood bar and overhead lighting that highlights the shelves holding their wine selection. Sit on their porch with a great glass of wine in hand and enjoy gorgeous views of the vineyard.

✦ **CELLARDOOR WINERY** in Lincolnville, Maine, is a few miles down the road from the center of Camden. Situated inside a renovated 1790s dairy barn, this winery is stunning. It features reclaimed hardwood floors, a spacious loft with exposed beams, and a tasting area that overlooks the hills of the 68-acre vineyard. Bring a picnic lunch or cheese and crackers and sit outside sipping wines to tempt every palate. Their winery has a bright and airy gift store that features wine accessories, handmade wine glasses, gourmet foods, kitchenware, and cookbooks.

✦ **NASHOBA WINERY**, located in Bolton, Massachusetts, produces numerous varieties of wine, including their own distinct Strawberry Rhubarb. Their stunning bright and spacious winery gift store features over a dozen estate and fruit wines, microbrews, and kitchenware. Their top seller of Cranberry Apple offers a sweet yet tart flavor that pairs perfectly with grilled salmon or shrimp. If you are a fan of brandy, make sure to try their apple brandy.

✦ **HARDWICK VINEYARD AND WINERY**, located in Hardwick, Massachusetts, grows six varieties of French hybrid grapes on their 150-acre farm, producing over 3,500 gallons of wine every year. One of their most popular varieties is called Massetts, which is a blend of locally grown tart cranberries and their own farm-grown grapes. Two of my favorites are their Yankee Girl Blush, which the vineyard describes as summer in a bottle, and the Quabbin Native, a sweet grape and raspberry wine. Host your party in their timber-frame barn, or join them for a tasting Friday through Sunday as they celebrate history and local agriculture.

BLACKBERRY & BLUEBERRY SPIKED LEMONADE

This refreshing berry lemonade is inspired by my father's love of blackberry brandy. What better way to quench your thirst than with blueberries and a splash of lemon, with the extra bonus of enjoying each other's company after a hard day on the farm?

Serves 12 to 14

2 CUPS SIMPLE SYRUP*

1 CUP FRESHLY SQUEEZED LEMON JUICE

2 CUPS BLUEBERRIES, PLUS MORE FOR GARNISH

1 (9.6-OUNCE) BOTTLE GUAVA NECTAR

1 1/2 CUPS BLACKBERRY BRANDY

1 (750 ML) BOTTLE INEXPENSIVE WHITE WINE (CHARDONNAY OR SAUVIGNON BLANC), CHILLED

LEMON SLICES, FOR GARNISH

In a blender, combine the simple syrup, lemon juice, blueberries, and guava nectar until the berries are pureed. Pour the blueberry mixture, brandy, and wine into a glass or plastic drink dispenser, adjusting the alcohol as you see fit. Add lemon slices and blueberries for garnish. Serve cold with plenty of ice.

*Make your own simple syrup by boiling 1 1/2 cups water with 1 1/2 cups sugar.

SANGRIA

This Sangria recipe—the perfect mix of sweet, tangy, and refreshing—will be a hit at your next backyard party. For the simple syrup, boil together equal parts sugar and water.

Serves 12 to 14

1 (750 ML) BOTTLE INEXPENSIVE WHITE WINE (CHARDONNAY OR SAUVIGNON BLANC)

1 (9.6-OUNCE) BOTTLE GUAVA NECTAR

½ CUP BRANDY

¾ CUP TRIPLE SEC

1 CUP SIMPLE SYRUP

1 CAN GINGER ALE

SLICED RED AND GREEN APPLES, FOR SERVING

ORANGE SLICES, FOR SERVING

Combine all the liquids together, adjusting alcohol as you see fit. Serve cold in a glass or plastic drink dispenser with sliced fruit and plenty of ice.

RASPBERRY WINE SPRITZER

Nothing says summer to me more than tart, sweet raspberries. Add raspberry ginger ale to wine, and you'll have a wonderfully refreshing end to your day. This drink pairs perfectly with grilled chicken, salads, and fish.

Serves 4 to 6

¾ CUP RASPBERRIES

1 (1.5-LITER) BOTTLE WHITE WINE (CHARDONNAY OR SAUVIGNON BLANC), CHILLED

3–4 CANS RASPBERRY GINGER ALE

JUICE OF 1 LIME

JUICE OF 1 LEMON

ORANGE SLICES, FOR GARNISH

To make the raspberry ice cubes, place a handful of raspberries into the bottom of either a muffin pan or mini Bundt cake pan. Cover the berries with about 1 inch of water; set in the freezer for 1 hour. Add a few more raspberries to each cup and fill to the top with water. Place back in the freezer until completely set.

To make the spritzer, pour the wine, ginger ale, lime juice, and lemon juice into a glass or plastic drink dispenser, adding raspberry ice cubes and orange slices for garnish. Serve cold in wine glasses.

BOURBON-HONEY BARBEQUE SAUCE

This tangy and sweet barbeque sauce is sure to become a grilling favorite, as it is a delightful combination of sweet and spicy with a kick of bourbon. Once you make your own homemade barbeque sauce, you'll never buy any at the grocery store again.

Makes 4 cups

½ CUP WATER

½ CUP BOURBON

¾ CUP CIDER VINEGAR

½ CUP GRANULATED SUGAR

½ CUP MOLASSES

¾ CUP HONEY

¼ CUP FIRMLY PACKED BROWN SUGAR

½ TEASPOON FRESHLY GROUND BLACK PEPPER

½ TEASPOON GROUND SMOKED PAPRIKA

½ TEASPOON GROUND CAYENNE PEPPER

½ TEASPOON KOSHER SALT

¾ CUP TOMATO PASTE

1 TEASPOON GARLIC POWDER

1 TABLESPOON ONION POWDER

In a large saucepan over medium heat, whisk together all of the ingredients. Bring to a boil, stirring continuously. Allow the mixture to simmer for 5 to 10 minutes, until thickened. Transfer to a glass jar and refrigerate for up to 4 weeks. Or process in a water bath to make it shelf stable.

HARD CIDER AND BROWN SUGAR-MARINATED CHICKEN

You'll love this marinade for chicken due to its wonderful sweet yet savory flavor that leaves chicken extremely moist. Use leftovers (if you're lucky enough to have any) on a fresh-from-the-garden salad or homemade pizza.

Serves 4 to 6

2 POUNDS BONELESS, SKINLESS CHICKEN BREAST

½ CUP HARD APPLE CIDER

¼ CUP FIRMLY PACKED BROWN SUGAR

2 TABLESPOONS MOLASSES

2 TEASPOONS KOSHER SALT

2 TEASPOONS BLACK PEPPER

2 TEASPOONS GROUND MUSTARD

1 TEASPOON SMOKED PAPRIKA

1 TABLESPOON BUTTER

1 TABLESPOON VEGETABLE OIL

Cut boneless chicken breasts into strips about 1 to 2 inches wide. Place the cider, brown sugar, molasses, salt, pepper, mustard, and paprika into a ziplock bag. Add the chicken to the bag and allow to marinate in the refrigerator for 2 to 4 hours. Remove the chicken from the marinade, discarding marinade. Warm the butter and oil in a grill pan over medium-high heat. Grill each side of chicken until fully cooked, 4 to 5 minutes. Remove the chicken from the pan and allow to rest on a plate for a few minutes. Serve

FRENCH ONION SOUP

This soup is great for a cold, rainy day or to warm you up from a long New England winter. It also pairs well with a salad for a simple dinner. You can even make a batch and freeze it in plastic 1-quart deli containers, which helps make dinner easy when you don't have time.

Serves 4

½ CUP (1 STICK) UNSALTED BUTTER

2 TABLESPOONS OLIVE OIL

4 LARGE VIDALIA ONIONS, SLICED

1 TABLESPOON HONEY

½ CUP SHERRY

½ CUP APPLE CIDER

4 CUPS BEEF BROTH

KOSHER SALT AND FRESHLY GROUND BLACK PEPPER

2 TABLESPOONS BALSAMIC VINEGAR

FRENCH BAGUETTE OR ITALIAN BREAD

1 CUP SHREDDED MOZZARELLA OR PIZZA CHEESE BLEND

1 TABLESPOON DRIED PARSLEY

In a 4-quart pot, melt the butter and olive oil over medium heat. Add the sliced onions and honey; cook over low heat for about 30 minutes, or until the onions are soft and translucent. Make sure not to brown the onions. Add the sherry, apple cider, and beef broth; season with salt and pepper to taste, and stir. Allow the mixture to simmer over low to medium heat for about 30 more minutes. Add the balsamic vinegar and stir. Taste, and season with more salt and pepper if needed.

Preheat the oven broiler. Slice the bread into 1-inch-thick pieces. Place the bread on a baking pan and toast in the oven until just lightly golden brown, about 10 minutes. Ladle soup into ovenproof bowls or crocks, leaving a little space for bread. Place the toasted bread pieces on top of the crocks of soup. Sprinkle with cheese. Place under preheated broiler for about 5 minutes. Do not take your eyes off the bowls, or the topping may burn. Sprinkle with parsley and serve.

HOMEGROWN

RAISING YOUR
OWN FOOD

I have vivid memories of being in my family's vegetable garden from a very young age. I typically had on overalls, and my strawberry blonde hair was pulled into pigtails. My dad took me along when I was little to get our Troy-Bilt Rototiller in Troy, New York. He would walk behind the rototiller with a five-gallon bucket hanging off the handle to collect the rocks and stones kicked up as he tilled the garden to prepare it for the season's planting. My dad always wore dark blue dungarees, steel-toe boots, a robin's-egg blue work shirt, and red suspenders.

Growing a garden with the assistance of your children may be one of the best lessons you can teach them. Many kids today just assume that food comes from the grocery store. But do they realize that without our farms and orchards, we wouldn't have fresh foods to eat? Educate your children on where food comes from, while reminding them to appreciate the simple things in life. Working in a garden is a great way to help them learn the importance of preserving our farms and open land for future generations.

For your child's next birthday party, instead of traditional favors, send kids home with little "green" garden kits, filled with garden tools and seeds, plus information about organic and natural gardening practices. Many gardening tools and buckets that are made from recycled products can be purchased. (Even beach toys and toy trucks made from recycled milk jugs and saw dust can be bought; check out *www.greentoys.com*.) These kits encourage kids and parents alike to unwind and slow down by heading outside to enjoy the healthy benefits of gardening and yard work. Let kids learn how hard work pays off with the sweet reward of enjoying something they grew. Spend a little less time playing video games or watching television to create more family time. It is tremendously important for children to spend time with their parents and grandparents learning life's simple lessons.

Involve children with daily age-appropriate tasks for maintaining a family garden, such as planting seeds and weeding. You'll know whether or not your child should handle an item such as scissors or garden shears, but be willing to let them try new things. Children absorb information like sponges, and through your example, they will ultimately achieve good values, be respectful of others, and learn the goodness of outdoor life.

Gardening is such a simple and rewarding process. Plant a tiny seed in rich, fertile soil, water and care for it, then watch that seed transform into a full-grown plant that provides a wonderful harvest. With a little hard work, dirty hands, and maybe bare feet, you and your children can connect on a level that is tremendously meaningful. Gardening is such an amazing and simple process, yet it's also very rewarding.

✦ **COMSTOCK, FERRE & CO.** in Wethersfield, Connecticut, is one of the oldest continuously operating seed companies in the United States. Established in 1811 by James Lockwood Belden as the Wethersfield Seed Gardens, the company was expanded when Franklin Comstock and his son, William, succeeded Belden and were later joined by Henry Ferre. William Comstock brought great innovation and growth to the seed industry. Today, customers will find rows of vintage oak rocker bins and tin-lined oak drawers holding their heirloom seed stock. The store has original wood floors and a rustic smell in the air. It also is really a great place to visit with your children and family. The Gettle family has recently taken over the company to restore it to its original glory, working hard to search the world for heirloom seeds. Heirloom seeds help preserve our history and provide good, wholesome fruits and vegetables. This store is just like I remember it as a young child—simple and homegrown.

Take a drive to the rolling hills of Litchfield, Connecticut, from April to mid-May to see hundreds of thousands of daffodils in bloom at **LAUREL RIDGE FOUNDATION**. Remy and Virginia Morosani moved to the area in 1941 and had a pasture across from their home that was too rocky to be used as a hay field. In the fall of 1941, they planted approximately 10,000 daffodil bulbs. Each spring they dig up the areas with over-clustered bulbs and in the fall replant them in another area. They originally started with two acres and now span fifteen acres. The natural landscape of gently rolling hills, fields, and aged stone walls overlook a small lake. There is no charge to visitors and it is an incredible photo opportunity for the family.

✦ **CRICKET HILL GARDEN** in Thomaston, Connecticut, is a plant nursery established in 1989 featuring seven acres of fluffy peonies. From May to mid-June, soak up the sweet, heavenly smells of all the peonies flowering at the nursery. Pale ballet pink, snowy white, and sweet sugarplum-colored peonies adorn the lush landscape. They work hard to develop and cultivate peony plants that will grow well in your gardens.

Drive up the coast of Maine during early to mid-June and view the amazing, vibrant colors of the flowering lupine. Vibrant, rich hues of purple, lavender, pink, and blue cover the fields on the jewel coast. Purchase seeds that have been collected from those lupine plants and bring them home to plant in your own gardens. Lupine is a wonderful, naturalizing perennial that loves full sun and well-drained soil. During late July and into August, you can also gather and absorb the ripe flavors of freshly picked wild blueberries. There is nothing quite like their taste—a juicy punch of flavor in a small package. Enjoy a scrumptious lunch accompanied by a bottle of locally made blueberry wine while overlooking the salty sea waves splashing against the rocky coast of Maine. Several of my favorite spots are Ogunquit, Kennebunk, and Camden, Maine.

GARDENING TIPS

CREATE A COMPOST PILE WITH LEAVES, GRASS CLIPPINGS, VEGETABLE PEELS, EGGSHELLS, COFFEE GROUNDS, STRAW, AND DEAD WEEDS. Compost is a wonderful natural and earthy fertilizer for your gardens or lawn. All you need is to fence in a small area of the yard or purchase a composting kit at a local gardening or hardware store. By diverting organic materials from landfills or incinerators, you are benefiting everyone—preserving our land, air, and water. Take a pitchfork and turn the pile over every once in a while; this adds air and helps the material breakdown process. If you can't make a compost pile, a company named Cockadoodle DOO produces a great natural fertilizer. The company also offers organic topsoil and weed control for your lawn as well as potting soil mix, which is completely organic and a great source of nutrients for a wide variety of plants.

For home gardeners, as well as commercial farms and greenhouses, you can send your soil to the University of Connecticut in Storrs, Connecticut (*www.soiltest.uconn.edu*), and they will analyze it for fertility. They then make suggestions for fertilizer based on the types of plants you'll be growing. The University of Connecticut has a goal to reach out to gardeners and educate them about wise soil management and fertilizing practices.

RECYCLE RAINWATER FOR USE IN YOUR GARDENS. Cut a hole in the lid of large covered barrels and place them under your gutters to collect rainwater. It's a natural way to utilize Mother Nature's many gifts.

SAVE SPACE AND GROW VINES UPWARD. You can purchase wooden stakes or bamboo pieces to make tremendous trellises for trailing plants. You can grow bamboo in your own garden; just be aware that it can be very invasive. Plants such as pickling cucumbers, gourds, squash, and beans will grab onto the structure and save on space by growing upwards. You can also use bamboo pieces to help support tomatoes, or simply purchase tomato cages. By keeping tomatoes upright and off the ground, diseases will be prevented, the fruit will not go bad as quickly, and more tomatoes will be produced. They will also ripen more evenly. Tie the plants up as they grow with baling twine or a natural material. If using tomato cages, place them over the plants when they are young, helping to keep them even more upright.

MULCH YOUR GARDENS TO HELP REDUCE WEEDS, CONTROL EROSION, AND KEEP MOISTURE IN THE SOIL. Use grass clippings, straw, or hay to mulch gardens. (When using hay, ask for the second or third cutting, so it doesn't have seeds.) Mulching your garden will help maintain the moisture level, save water, and keep the painstaking task of weeding to a minimum.

Every fall our children and I plant daffodil and tulip bulbs to add more color and beauty to our property. With this task, the kids learn to follow directions, help out mom and dad, use garden tools, measure depths, and simply have fun. During the winter, I dump the cooled ashes from our fireplace into our annual garden and till them into the soil in the spring. When spring arrives, the tulips poke through the soil to reach up and grab the warmth of the sun, and in a few short weeks, they emerge with radiant beauty. As the plants grow, I teach my children to identify each variety.

Just as the tulips and daffodils start to push their way out of the soil and towards the warm sunlight, we rake out the leaves and mulch the gardens. We use natural double-ground bark mulch in our perennial gardens to reduce erosion, maintain moisture, and reduce weeds. It also makes the gardens look perfectly manicured. The kids and I load up the wheelbarrow or lawn mower trailer and spread the mulch carefully among the perennials. As raindrops mist in the air, gathering and collecting on cupped leaves, the plants will soak up the water deep into their roots, which will help them expand in growth.

In the late spring and into summer, as the soil warms up and the danger of frost disappears, we plant colorful annuals. Plant dahlias along the edge of your garden and they will make the perfect cut flower later on. Sunflowers, marigolds and zinnias are very simple to grow from seed placed directly into the soil. They make wonderful cut flowers as well.

We teach our children to help deadhead the blooms on our annuals. This means that we remove any spent flower blooms, encouraging new flower buds to grow. When you deadhead the older blooms, the plant will put energy into making new blooms rather than producing seeds. The more you do this, the more the plant will flower. Petunias will provide an enormous amount of continuous blooms all summer long if you deadhead regularly. The same applies to geraniums, zinnias, verbena, lantana, marigolds, and dahlias. Hummingbirds and butterflies come back year after year to enjoy the sweet flavors of the nectar and the bright, colorful blooms of annuals. They particularly like bee balm, stargazer lilies, phlox, and petunias.

As springs warms into early summer, we till the dark soil, preparing to plant tomato, eggplant, and pepper plants. For corn, we sow several rows of seed to begin with. Then, a week or so later, we plant a few more, so when we're done picking the first rows, there's more on the way. This ensures that each week, we have fresh sweet corn to pick. Planting more than one row also allows the corn to pollinate.

For lettuce and other cool-weather crops, such as peas, broccoli, spinach, and kale, we plant as early as we can and then again as the weather approaches cooler fall temperatures. Wax beans and green beans are simple to grow; just remember not to pick them while wet, or they will end up with rust-colored spots. Rhubarb is relatively simple to grow too; it comes up faithfully every year with little fuss. Add it to fresh ripe raspberries for the perfect taste of sweet and sour in jams and pies. When picking rhubarb, simply reach down and gently pluck the stem out of the ground. Remember to remove the leaves with a sharp knife, and add them to your compost pile, as they are poisonous and should not be eaten.

When growing pumpkins, you can pluck the other flower blooms off the vine to make one individual fruit get all the attention. That single pumpkin will grow larger because it's not sharing nutrients with the rest of the pumpkins on its vine. Remember to gently rotate the pumpkins as they grow and ripen; this will prevent them from being flat on one side and help them to ripen evenly. If you have a certain jack-o'-lantern design in mind, you can tie a rope around the center of the pumpkin to coax it into a desired shape. You can also score faces into the pumpkin, so you can carve it out with greater ease later.

✦ SHORTT'S FARM & GARDEN CENTER purveys landscaping essentials and organic foods, as well as advice on gardening. Located in Sandy Hook, Connecticut, they are the perfect farm stand to pick up organically grown lettuce, tomatoes, squash, broccoli, and sweet corn as well as other organic foods and local honey. Stop by Sandy Hook's organic farmers market to see them and other farmers committed to providing the freshest naturally grown produce around.

✦ FLOWER POWER FARMS in East Windsor, Connecticut, offers a huge assortment of annuals and perennials grown right on their farm. Flowering hanging baskets and large pots of annuals are bursting and overflowing with splashes of color. The largest retail garden center in northern Connecticut, they have over two acres of greenhouses and four acres of outdoor production. Everything is perfectly labeled, so you know what type of plant it is and what type of growing environment that plant prefers. You'll find a wonderful selection of potting soil, mulch, pots, and other gardening necessities at this gorgeous farm stand.

GOAT CHEESE SALAD WITH FRESH STRAWBERRIES

This simple salad reminds me of summers spent on the coast of Maine.

Serves 2

1 CUP BABY GREENS

THINLY SLICED ONION

4–5 GRAPE TOMATOES

2 TABLESPOONS SHREDDED CARROTS

2 FRESH STRAWBERRIES, SLICED

2 TABLESPOONS CHOPPED PECANS

3 TABLESPOONS BALSAMIC VINAIGRETTE

1 LARGE EGG

¼ CUP MILK

¼ CUP SEASONED BREAD CRUMBS

¼ CUP ALL-PURPOSE FLOUR

2–3 SLICES FRESH GOAT CHEESE

1 TABLESPOON BUTTER

Make the salad by tossing together the greens, onion as desired, tomatoes, carrots, strawberries, pecans, and balsamic vinaigrette in a large bowl.

Prepare an egg wash by adding the egg and milk to a flat container, beating until combined. Place the bread crumbs and flour into separate flat containers. Roll the goat cheese slices in the flour, then in the egg wash, and lastly in the bread crumbs.

Heat a skillet over medium heat and melt the butter. Cook the goat cheese until the bread crumb coating is just lightly golden. Serve over the prepared salad.

HONEY BALSAMIC VINAIGRETTE DRESSING

Homemade salad dressing eliminates any preservatives or additives. Add a little fresh lemon or orange zest for added citrusy oomph.

Makes about 1¼ cups

1 TABLESPOON DIJON MUSTARD

2 TABLESPOONS HONEY

1 TEASPOON FRESHLY SQUEEZED LEMON JUICE

¼ CUP APPLE CIDER

½ CUP BALSAMIC VINEGAR

¼ CUP OLIVE OIL

KOSHER SALT AND FRESHLY GROUND BLACK PEPPER

Into a pint Mason jar, add the mustard, honey, lemon juice, apple cider, vinegar, and olive oil; season to taste with salt and pepper. Cover tightly with a lid and shake until it's thoroughly combined. Store in the refrigerator for up to 1 month.

CARAMELIZED PEAR SALAD

This salad is excellent in late summer, throughout the autumn season, and even in winter. The flavors make a wonderful medley together and the pear melts in your mouth. Caramelized pecans add a little crunch and texture to this delicious salad.

Serves 2

1 BOSC PEAR, HALVED

1 TABLESPOON GRANULATED SUGAR

1 TABLESPOON BUTTER

2 CUPS BABY GREENS

¼ CUP RED CABBAGE, SHREDDED

¼ CUP SHREDDED CARROT

¼ CUP CRUMBLED GORGONZOLA OR BLUE CHEESE

THINLY SLICED ONION

1 HEIRLOOM TOMATO, THICKLY SLICED

2 TABLESPOONS CARAMELIZED PECANS (PAGE 127)

Preheat the oven to 350 degrees F.

Dip the cut side of both pear halves into a shallow bowl of sugar. Over low to medium heat, melt the butter in a small ovenproof sauté pan. Put the sugar-dipped side of the pear down into the pan and caramelize. Finish off in the oven for about 10 minutes to soften the pear further. Combine remaining ingredients in a bowl. Top the salad with the pear halves.

CARAMELIZED PECANS

These are very simple to make at home. Add them to homemade granola, toss on a salad, or eat as is for a snack. They are also wonderful in homemade brownies.

2 CUPS MAPLE SYRUP

4 CUPS PECAN HALVES

Preheat the oven to 200 degrees F. Grease a sheet pan and set aside.

In a 4-quart pot over low to medium heat, heat the maple syrup to 245 degrees F. Use a candy thermometer to check the temperature. Once it has reached 245 degrees F, remove the pot from the heat. Using a wooden spoon or spatula, stir the nuts into the syrup to coat them.

Place the nuts onto the sheet pan and bake for about 1 hour, or until they are fully dry. Place the nuts in a glass jar and keep in a cool dry place. They have about a 6- to 8-month shelf life.

STRAWBERRY-RASPBERRY POPSICLES

Making ice pops at home is super easy, and your children will devour them. Make extra ahead of time to be ready for a picnic or after a kids' baseball game.

Serves 6 to 8

2 CUPS FRESH RASPBERRIES

2 CUPS HALVED FRESH STRAWBERRIES

1/2 CUP GRANULATED SUGAR

1/4 CUP FRESHLY SQUEEZED LEMON JUICE

3/4 CUP WATER

In a blender or food processor, puree all ingredients until smooth. Set a fine-mesh strainer over a medium bowl and strain out the seeds, pressing the mixture through with a rubber spatula. Transfer the liquid into a large measuring cup and pour into ice pop molds. Cover and insert the wood craft sticks. Freeze until firm. When they are fully frozen, run the bottom of the mold under warm water to easily remove the ice pops. Eat immediately or put into freezer-safe bags to enjoy later.

TRIPLE BERRY PRESERVES

Gather berries from your garden or the local farm. Make these preserves in small batches, or freeze the berries and make a big batch later in the season. Making homemade jam lets you control the ingredients, and nothing could be tastier.

Makes 12 (8-ounce) jars

2½ CUPS RASPBERRIES

2½ CUPS STRAWBERRIES

2½ CUPS BLUEBERRIES

7 CUPS GRANULATED SUGAR, DIVIDED

1 (1.75-OUNCE) PACKAGE FRUIT PECTIN

1 TABLESPOON FRESHLY SQUEEZED LEMON JUICE

BUTTER, OPTIONAL

In a 6- to 8-quart saucepan, cook the raspberries, strawberries, and blueberries over low to medium heat until soft. Lightly smash the fruit with a potato masher. Meanwhile, prepare a boiling water canner. Heat the jars and lids in simmering water until ready for use. Do not boil. Set bands aside.

In a large stock pot, combine 2 cups sugar with the pectin. Add the lemon juice and sugar-pectin mixture to the berries. Over high heat, bring the mixture to a full rolling boil that cannot be stirred down, stirring frequently with a wooden spoon. Boil for 1 minute. Add the remaining 5 cups sugar immediately, and bring back up to a hard boil for 1 minute, stirring constantly. Remove from heat. Skim foam if necessary; a touch of butter will help eliminate any foam.

Ladle hot preserves into hot jars, leaving ½ inch headspace. Wipe the rim with a clean, damp paper towel. Center the lid on the jar. Apply the band until the fit is fingertip tight. Process jars in a boiling water canner for 10 minutes, adjusting for altitude. Remove the jars and allow to cool. I use a pair of rubber-tipped tongs to easily handle hot jars. Check the lids for seal after 24 hours. The lid should not flex up and down when the center is pressed. Store jars in a cool, dry place.

PEACH-RASPBERRY JAM

Fresh-picked tart raspberries marry with sweet, juicy summer peaches to make this jam—one of my absolute favorites—the perfect addition to toast, bagels, or scones.

Makes 12 (8-ounce) jars

3 CUPS RASPBERRIES

4 CUPS SLICED PEACHES

7 1/2 CUPS GRANULATED SUGAR, DIVIDED

1 (1.75-OUNCE) PACKAGE FRUIT PECTIN

2 TABLESPOONS FRESHLY SQUEEZED LEMON JUICE

BUTTER, OPTIONAL

In a 6- to 8-quart saucepan, cook the raspberries and peaches over low to medium heat until soft. Lightly smash the fruit with a potato masher. Meanwhile, prepare a boiling water canner. Heat the jars and lids in simmering water until ready for use. Do not boil. Set bands aside.

In a large stock pot, combine 2 cups sugar with the pectin. Add the lemon juice and sugar-pectin mixture to the berries. Over high heat, bring the mixture to a full rolling boil that cannot be stirred down, stirring frequently with a wooden spoon. Boil for 1 minute. Add the remaining 5 1/2 cups sugar immediately, and bring back up to a hard boil for 1 minute, stirring constantly. Remove from heat. Skim foam if necessary; a touch of butter will help eliminate any foam.

Ladle hot preserves into hot jars, leaving 1/2 inch headspace. Wipe the rim with a clean, damp paper towel. Center the lid on the jar. Apply the band until the fit is fingertip tight. Process jars in a boiling water canner for 10 minutes, adjusting for altitude. Remove the jars and allow to cool. Check the lids for seal after 24 hours. The lid should not flex up and down when the center is pressed. Store jars in a cool, dry place.

FARMHOUSE SWEET & TANGY PICKLES

Sweet yet tangy pickles are the perfect addition to your summer sandwich. Pickles are relatively easy to make, and there is nothing better than homemade. We grow cucumbers on a trellis made of chicken wire in our garden to condense space. Be sure to use a 5-gallon food-grade plastic bucket, which can be picked up at your local bakery; bakeries purchase products in them and are happy to give them away.

Makes 24 (8-ounce) jars

24 CUPS SLICED CUCUMBERS (¼ INCH THICK)

½ CUP KOSHER SALT

1 LARGE ONION, DICED

½ RED PEPPER, DICED

6 CUPS CIDER VINEGAR

2 CUPS WHITE VINEGAR

6 CUPS GRANULATED SUGAR

½ TABLESPOON TURMERIC POWDER

1 TEASPOON MUSTARD SEED

1 TEASPOON CELERY SEED

In a 5-gallon food-grade bucket, add the sliced cucumbers, salt, onion, and pepper. Stir so the salt is evenly distributed. Cover the cucumber mixture with a clean tea towel. Place a few inches of ice on top of the towel. Allow to sit for 3 to 4 hours in a cool place.

Drain the cucumbers. Make the brine for the pickles by bringing the cider and white vinegars, sugar, and spices to a boil in a large pot over high heat.

Meanwhile, sterilize your jars in a 16-quart canning pot. Place the cucumbers, onions, and peppers into the jars. Using a wide-mouth funnel, ladle hot pickling liquid over top of the cucumbers, leaving ½ inch headspace. Remove any air bubbles. Wipe the rim with a clean, damp paper towel. Center the lid on the jar. Apply the band until the fit is fingertip tight. Add the jars to a water bath for 15 minutes, adjusting for altitude. Remove from the water bath. Allow to cool completely on the counter for 24 hours. For best flavor, let stand for 3 to 4 weeks before enjoying. Store the jars in a cool, dry place for up to 1 year.

RUSTIC APPLESAUCE

Making applesauce at home is wonderfully simple. Plus, you control all the ingredients for this kid favorite that is a combination of tart apples and sweet maple syrup. Grab a bushel of seconds from the local orchard; it will save you money and still give you plenty of fresh flavor.

Makes 12 to 14 (8-ounce) jars

4–5 POUNDS SEASONAL TART APPLES

1 CUP WATER

¾ CUP PACKED BROWN SUGAR

¼ CUP FRESHLY SQUEEZED LEMON JUICE

½ CUP MAPLE SYRUP

1 TABLESPOON GROUND CINNAMON

½ TEASPOON GROUND NUTMEG

1 TEASPOON KOSHER SALT

Wash and cut up the apples into quarters. There is no need to peel or core them. Add the apples to a large pot with the water and cover. Cook apples over medium heat until they are soft and falling apart. Using a stainless steel food mill, place the cooked apples into the mill a few cups at a time and rotate the handle to mash the apples through into a large clean pot. Turn the handle clockwise, then turn counterclockwise to scrape the bottom of the mill. Empty the apple peels and seeds into your garbage or compost pile. Continue this process until all of the cooked apples are processed through the food mill.

Place the puree in a large pan and add the sugar, lemon juice, maple syrup, and spices; stir to combine. Cook the applesauce over medium heat until thickened, about 10 minutes.

Meanwhile, sterilize the jars.

Keep the applesauce simmering over low heat. Ladle hot applesauce into hot jars, leaving ½ inch headspace. Wipe the rim with a clean, damp paper towel. Center the lid on the jar. Apply the bands until fit is fingertip tight. Process jars in a boiling water canner for 15 minutes, adjusting for altitude. Remove the jars and allow to cool. Check the lids for seal after 24 hours. The lid should not flex up and down when the center is pressed. Store jars in a cool, dry place.

PICKLED SWEET PEPPERS

These are truly one of my absolute favorites. Put them on an egg, cheese, and sausage biscuit for breakfast, a BLT with heirloom tomatoes, or your favorite sandwich. I use several different colors of sweet peppers, which looks so pretty in the jar.

Makes 8 (16-ounce) jars

1 TABLESPOON KOSHER SALT

6 CUPS CIDER VINEGAR

2 CUPS WHITE VINEGAR

4 CUPS WATER

6 CUPS GRANULATED SUGAR

8–10 CLOVES GARLIC, SMASHED

1/2 TABLESPOON TURMERIC POWDER

1 TABLESPOON WHOLE PEPPERCORNS

1 TEASPOON MUSTARD SEED

1 TEASPOON CELERY SEED

41/2–5 POUNDS RED, GREEN AND ORANGE SWEET PEPPERS, SLICED 1/4-INCH THICK

1 LARGE ONION, HALVED AND SLICED THINLY

In a large pot, make the brine. Place the salt, cider and white vinegars, water, sugar, garlic, and spices in a large pan and bring to a boil over medium to high heat.

Sterilize your jars in a 16-quart canning pot. Place the sliced peppers and onions into the jars. Press down to compact and make sure you have plenty of peppers and onions in each jar, as they will rise up to the surface during the processing. Using a wide-mouth funnel, ladle hot pickling brine over top of the peppers and onions, leaving 1/2 inch headspace. Remove any air bubbles. Wipe the rim with a clean, damp paper towel. Center the lid on the jar. Apply the band until the fit is fingertip tight. Place the jars in a water bath and process for 15 minutes, adjusting for altitude. Remove from the water bath. Allow to cool completely on the counter for 24 hours. For best flavor, let stand for 3 to 4 weeks before enjoying. Store the jars in a cool, dry place for up to 1 year.

HARVEST PUMPKIN BUTTER

Pumpkin butter is a favorite in New England. Spread it on scones, toast, or an English muffin for a delicious breakfast. Note that the USDA recommends not canning pumpkin at home because it is too dense.

Makes 2 pint containers

3 CUPS MASHED FRESH OR CANNED PUMPKIN

1/2 CUP MAPLE SYRUP

1/3 CUP FIRMLY PACKED BROWN SUGAR

1 1/2 TEASPOONS FRESHLY SQUEEZED LEMON JUICE

1 TEASPOON GROUND CINNAMON

1/2 TEASPOON GROUND NUTMEG

1/2 TEASPOON GROUND GINGER

1/4 TEASPOON GROUND CLOVES

1/4 TEASPOON KOSHER SALT

In a large saucepan over medium heat, mix all of the ingredients together. Stir with a wooden spoon frequently, taking care not to burn the mixture. Heat until thickened, about 20 minutes. Ladle into jars, allow to cool, then refrigerate for up to 2 weeks.

FARMHOUSE PUMPKIN POUND CAKE

I created this yummy spice cake recipe a few years back, and it's turned into one of our personal favorites. The maple adds a unique depth of flavor. This cake is extremely moist and the perfect treat right out of the oven with pats of fresh butter. I line 3 loaf pans with paper liners to help easily slide the cake out of the pans.

Makes 3 loaves or 1 Bundt cake

2 CUPS ALL-PURPOSE FLOUR

2 CUPS MASHED FRESH OR CANNED PUMPKIN

1 CUP VEGETABLE OIL

1 CUP GRANULATED SUGAR

1 CUP GRANULATED MAPLE SUGAR

4 LARGE EGGS

2 TEASPOONS BAKING SODA

1 TEASPOON KOSHER SALT

2 TEASPOONS GROUND CINNAMON

Preheat the oven to 350 degrees F. Grease 3 loaf pans or 1 Bundt cake pan; set aside.

In a large mixing bowl, combine all of the ingredients until thoroughly mixed, then pour batter into prepared pans. Bake for 55 to 60 minutes, or until a toothpick inserted in the center comes out clean. Allow to cool on baking racks, then remove from the pan(s).

APPLE FRITTERS

These remind me of all the wonderful old-fashioned fairs throughout the summer and early fall in New England. While growing up, we spent many hours at local fairs showing pigs and selling products from our farm. My father would often trade maple syrup with a local vendor for fresh apple fritters whenever the urge hit.

Makes about 24 small fritters

VEGETABLE SHORTENING

1¾ CUPS ALL-PURPOSE FLOUR

2 TABLESPOONS GRANULATED MAPLE SUGAR

2 TEASPOONS BAKING POWDER

1 TEASPOON KOSHER SALT

¾ CUP BUTTERMILK

2 LARGE EGGS

1 TEASPOON PURE VANILLA EXTRACT

1 TABLESPOON VEGETABLE OIL

2 TABLESPOONS PLUS ½ TEASPOON GROUND CINNAMON, DIVIDED

3 CUPS PEELED, CORED, AND FINELY CHOPPED APPLES

1 CUP GRANULATED SUGAR

In a large pot for frying, add vegetable shortening at about 3 inches deep. Preheat the shortening to about 370 degrees F. Line a baking sheet with paper towels and set aside.

In a large bowl, combine the flour, maple sugar, baking powder, and salt. Pour in the buttermilk, eggs, vanilla, oil and ½ teaspoon cinnamon. Stir with a wooden spoon or spatula until well blended. Fold in the chopped apples until they are evenly combined.

Using a tablespoon, drop the batter a spoonful at a time into the preheated oil. Fry for about 2 minutes on each side, until golden. Fry in small batches, so they do not overcrowd the pan. Remove the fritters from the hot oil and drain on the paper towel–lined baking sheet. Add the remaining 2 tablespoons cinnamon and sugar into a brown paper lunch bag. While the fritters are still warm, add them to the bag, fold over the top of the bag, and shake. Remove the fritters from the paper bag and enjoy warm.

YANKEE BACKYARD ENTERTAINING

SAVORING THE OUTDOORS

In the summer and fall evenings, we gather as a family around the fire pit outside to enjoy good food, each other's company, and incredible wine. Our children toast marshmallows over the glowing flames for s'mores. We have more fun entertaining when the time is spent under the glowing amber moon in our backyard. We enjoy local food and share laughter and conversation. We gather with friends and family simply because enjoying life helps lighten the stress of everyday craziness. Life passes quickly, so relish each and every moment.

While we prepare dinner on the grill, our children play fetch with our yellow Lab and swing on their play set. Laughing, enjoying nature, and playing are such important things to do. Children grow up so quickly; remember to let them be kids. Set up a tent in the backyard and enjoy a campout with the kids. Bodies tucked deep in a cozy sleeping bag enjoying the fresh outdoor air are what camping is all about.

Plan a simple, flavorful meal with fresh, local ingredients when inviting friends and family over. Try new recipes or stick with time-honored classics, like my pick of strawberry shortcake. Chill a bottle of locally produced wine, light the grill, and enjoy a flavorful meal with good company. Light beeswax candles around the pool and patio, relax, and just savor the moment. Listen to the peepers and tell each other stories. Sit back, stare at the stars, and enjoy the wonders of nature.

For a creative table setting, gather flowers that you grew or purchased into Mason jars, and surround them with beeswax or soy candles. I love to add aged terra-cotta pots to the table setting as well, which I fill with natural moss or blooming in-season plants. Fruit and fresh vegetables also make fabulous decorations. Fill large clear cylinder vases with heirloom tomatoes or unique varieties of gourds, eggplant, or apples to use as the centerpiece. I have found incredible Tiara glassware vintage vases at local yard sales. You could also use old wooden apple or wine crates instead of a vase.

Vintage drinking glasses are great substitutes for vases; check out Anchor Company for incredible ones. You can also find peanut butter glasses that date back to the 1950s when peanut butter was packaged in decorative glass-footed cups. Fill wide-mouth Mason jars with dried beans or coffee beans, then place an unscented votive inside the glass. The coffee beans add a subtle fragrance that will not overpower the smells of your food. Simplicity is the key to any great table setting. Using only one flower variety or monochromatic designs, you'll achieve tremendous results. Add a little candlelight for mood, ambience, and suspense.

During the winter, bring the outdoors inside and decorate with fragrant evergreens, such as white pine, white and blue spruce, cedar, and a wide variety of furs. The sprigs last a long time and add the spicy and warm aromas of the outdoors. Add pinecones for a beautiful natural look. You can also place cranberries in a vase, fill with water, and float a candle on top, which adds height as well as rich color. Or try using lemons, limes, kumquats, or Lady Gala apples in glass vases. Gather simple glass ornaments to add sparkle to your centerpieces or décor over the fireplace. You can also use non-breakable ornaments that mimic glass ones. Try inserting whole cloves into citrus fruit such as limes, lemons, and oranges, and then roll them in cinnamon. Hang them off the tree with natural rope or baling twine or place them in clear bowls. The fragrance of cinnamon and spices is warm and intense.

There are some wonderful winter activities to do with your kids. After a snowstorm, go outside for some fun in the freshly fallen snow by creating an amazing snowman and decorating him with an old scarf, branches for arms, a carrot nose, and coal for buttons on his belly. Take large pinecones and hang them by a string tied to the bottom so they hang upside down. Warm some peanut butter in the microwave, spread over the pinecones, and roll them in birdseed. These make a wonderful treat for the birds to enjoy during the cold months.

We also use pinecones to make the simplest Christmas ornaments. Attach a ribbon or a string to the bottom then apply glue and sprinkle with colorful glitter and allow to thoroughly dry. Salt dough ornaments are an inexpensive and simple way to make the prettiest handmade ornaments. Grandma and grandpa are sure to appreciate the time and effort the children put into something so personalized.

SWEET CORNBREAD

I love serving cornbread at a down-home, family-style dinner. Try serving it for your back-yard barbeque or during the winter with a hearty soup.

Makes 1 pan

2 CUPS YELLOW CORNMEAL

1 1/2 CUPS WHOLE MILK

2 CUPS ALL-PURPOSE FLOUR

1/2 CUP FIRMLY PACKED BROWN SUGAR

1/2 CUP GRANULATED SUGAR

1 TEASPOON KOSHER SALT

2 1/2 TEASPOONS BAKING POWDER

2 LARGE EGGS

2/3 CUP VEGETABLE OIL

BUTTER, FOR SERVING

Preheat the oven to 375 degrees F. Prepare a 9 1/2 x 11-inch baking pan with cooking spray and set aside.

In a medium bowl, soak the cornmeal in the milk for about 15 minutes. In a large bowl, combine the flour, brown and granulated sugars, salt, and baking powder. Mix in 1 egg at a time. Stir in the milk and cornmeal mixture and the vegetable oil.

Pour the batter into the prepared baking pan, and place on the middle rack of the oven. Bake for 30 to 35 minutes, until a toothpick inserted in center comes out clean. Allow to cool for 5 to 10 minutes. Serve with fresh butter.

STEAK DRY RUB

As soon as the spring sun melts away the last of the snow, we are ready to grill. We love to eat outside under the stars with the fire pit crackling away and fireflies dancing in the moonlight. During the winter, I use a cast-iron grill pan on our stovetop to achieve similar results. This dry rub is one of our favorite ways to prep a steak ready for the grill.

Makes 1 cup

½ CUP FIRMLY PACKED BROWN SUGAR

¼ CUP ALL-PURPOSE FLOUR

2 TEASPOONS GRANULATED GARLIC

1 TABLESPOON GRANULATED ONION

1 TABLESPOON DRY MUSTARD

2 TEASPOONS KOSHER SALT

2 TEASPOONS FRESHLY GROUND BLACK PEPPER

2 TEASPOONS GROUND PAPRIKA

1½ TEASPOONS GROUND NUTMEG

2 TEASPOONS GROUND GINGER

ZEST OF 1 LARGE LEMON

In a small bowl, mix together all of the ingredients.

To use, rub thoroughly onto both sides of the steak and allow the meat to absorb the flavors for at least 1 hour while refrigerated.

Preheat the grill. Grill steak for 4 to 5 minutes, then flip and grill the other side for the same amount of time, or until cooked through the way you like. This rub caramelizes on the meat and adds great grill marks. Let the steak rest for about 5 minutes after grilling, then slice and serve.

FRUIT PUNCH

We make this tangy and sweet fruit punch every holiday. It's refreshing and sure to turn into a holiday tradition for your family as well.

Serves 10 to 12

4 CUPS FRUIT PUNCH (SUCH AS KOOL-AID)

1 (12-OUNCE) CONTAINER FROZEN LEMONADE CONCENTRATE

1 (2-LITER) BOTTLE LEMON-LIME SODA

FRUIT ICE RING (BELOW)

In a punch bowl, combine fruit punch, frozen lemonade, and lemon-lime soda. Add plenty of ice or a fruit ice ring. Ladle servings into ice-filled glasses.

FRUIT ICE RING

My mom has served this ice ring at our family Christmas parties for as long as I can remember. It's simple to make and adds lots of texture and color to the holiday punch. We use fresh oranges and frozen fruit during the winter. If you're making this in the spring or summer, utilize fresh fruit.

Makes 1 large ice ring or several small ones

BUNDT PAN OR MINI BUNDT PANS

1 ORANGE, SLICED

1 CUP FROZEN BLUEBERRIES

1 CUP FROZEN RASPBERRIES

Fill a large Bundt pan or mini Bundt pans with a thin layer of water. Line with orange slices and frozen berries and place in the freezer for at least 1 hour. Once the water is frozen, continue to layer with water and more fruit until filled completely; freeze. Serve in a punch bowl or clear pitcher.

HEARTY SAUSAGE AND VEGETABLE SOUP

This soup is from the heart of our farm kitchen. My mom makes it during the fall and winter to warm us up. It's got an incredible depth of flavor, and we love it topped with freshly shredded sharp cheddar in a sourdough bread bowl.

Serves 4

2 TABLESPOONS OLIVE OIL

2 LARGE ONIONS, CHOPPED

2 LARGE GREEN OR RED BELL PEPPERS, CHOPPED

8–10 LINKS ITALIAN SAUSAGE

2 (10-OUNCE) CONTAINERS CHICKEN STOCK

2 CUPS WATER

1 TABLESPOON DRIED BASIL

2 TABLESPOONS ITALIAN SEASONING

1 (6-OUNCE) CAN TOMATO PASTE

1 (16-OUNCE) CAN DICED TOMATOES WITH LIQUID

1 (10-OUNCE) BAG FROZEN GREEN BEANS

1 (10-OUNCE) BAG FROZEN CORN

1 POUND PASTA (ELBOW MACARONI OR BOWTIES)

KOSHER SALT AND FRESHLY GROUND BLACK PEPPER

In a large Dutch oven, warm the olive oil over medium-high heat. Sauté the onions and peppers until onions are translucent. Add the sausage and cook until done. Remove the sausage, cut it into pieces, and return it to the pot. Add the chicken stock, water, basil, Italian seasoning, tomato paste, tomatoes, green beans, corn, and pasta. Season to taste with salt and pepper, and cook until the pasta is done, stirring occasionally.

POP'S BAKED BEANS

My grandmother said that my grandfather never measured anything while cooking. So in order to get this recipe, she stood careful watch over his shoulder while he made these baked beans. My grandfather insisted on using Jack Rabbit–brand beans.

Serves 6 to 8

1 (16-OUNCE) BAG NAVY BEANS, SOAKED OVERNIGHT

1 TEASPOON BAKING SODA

1/2–3/4 CUP MOLASSES

1/2 CUP FIRMLY PACKED BROWN SUGAR

1/2 CUP KETCHUP

1 TEASPOON DRY MUSTARD

6–8 SLICES THICK-CUT BACON, COOKED AND ROUGHLY CHOPPED

ONION POWDER

FRESHLY GROUND BLACK PEPPER

Preheat the oven to 350 degrees F.

Drain the water from the beans. Place the beans into a large pot, and cover with fresh water. Add the baking soda, and bring water to a boil over high heat. Continue to boil for about 10 minutes, removing the foam with a large serving spoon. Drain beans into a colander and rinse. Transfer beans into a large ovenproof pot and cover with warm water.

Add the molasses, brown sugar, ketchup, mustard, and bacon; season to taste with onion powder and pepper. Cook the beans for about 4 to 5 hours, or until beans get really dark in color and the sauce thickens. Check periodically; if the beans dry out during the cooking process, add more water.

→ The Bean Pot

So the story goes . . . my grandmother was always mad at my grandfather for having a small engine repair business in the garage and constantly having customers in the yard. So one day she got really mad and chucked the bean pot over the edge of the property where they dumped brush. My brother and I retrieved it and Grandma Rusin allowed me to keep the pot.

HERB-ROASTED CHICKEN

This wonderfully juicy chicken offers golden skin and flavorful meat. It works well with many root vegetables or even a sliced head of cabbage for added flavor. White wine is poured over the chicken before roasting. Like the old saying goes, if you wouldn't drink the wine, don't cook with it.

Serves 4

1 ROASTING CHICKEN (ABOUT 5–6 POUNDS)

¼ CUP (½ STICK) BUTTER, SOFTENED

½ TEASPOON ONION POWDER

2 TEASPOONS DRY MUSTARD

ZEST OF 1 LEMON

2 HEAPING TEASPOONS ITALIAN SEASONING

KOSHER SALT AND FRESHLY GROUND BLACK PEPPER

1 CUP WHITE WINE

1 (12-OUNCE) PACKAGE HERB-SEASONED BREAD STUFFING

6–8 RED POTATOES, CHOPPED

1 LARGE ONION, SLICED

1 (1-POUND) PACKAGE BABY CARROTS

Preheat the oven to 350 degrees F.

Remove giblets from the chicken and dispose. Place the chicken in the center of a large roasting pan. In a medium bowl, mix the butter with the onion powder, mustard, lemon zest, and Italian seasoning; season with salt and pepper. Use your fingers to rub the butter and herb mixture all over the chicken. Pour the wine over the chicken. Add the stuffing into the cavity of the chicken and place the potatoes, onions, and baby carrots around the chicken.

Place in the oven and bake until the instant pop-up thermometer pops up or the internal temperature reaches 165 degrees F, usually about 1 hour and 45 minutes. Baste the chicken periodically, adding more white wine if needed to keep the vegetables and chicken moist.

RUSTIC HERB POTATOES

Crispy on the outside and soft in the center, these potatoes are delicious and simple to make. Bacon adds a wonderful distinct flavor, and honey creates a tangy caramelized potato skin.

Serves 4

3 MEDIUM RED POTATOES

3 MEDIUM RUSSET POTATOES

3–4 SLICES THICK-CUT BACON, FINELY CHOPPED

1 SMALL ONION, FINELY CHOPPED

6 TABLESPOONS (¾ STICK) BUTTER, SLICED

3 TABLESPOONS OLIVE OIL

4 TABLESPOONS HONEY

1 TABLESPOON DRY MUSTARD

1 TEASPOON LEMON PEPPER

3 TABLESPOONS ITALIAN SEASONING

KOSHER SALT AND FRESHLY GROUND BLACK PEPPER

Preheat the oven to 400 degrees F.

Wash the potatoes and cut them into $\frac{1}{4}$-inch to $\frac{1}{2}$-inch pieces. Add potatoes to a $9\frac{1}{2}$ x 12-inch metal baking pan. Add the bacon, onion, butter, olive oil, honey, mustard, lemon pepper, and Italian seasoning into the pan with potatoes; season with salt and pepper to taste. Mix everything together with a spatula. Bake the potatoes uncovered for about 45 minutes to 1 hour, or until golden brown. Stir the potatoes every once in a while to prevent burning.

TEXAS TOAST BLTS

Bacon, lettuce, and tomato sandwiches are a quick and delicious option for lunch or dinner. There is nothing quite like picking a plump, juicy heirloom tomato off the vine from your garden and enjoying it on this yummy sandwich. For a quicker clean-up, place bacon strips on a baking sheet and place in a 400-degree oven until crisp.

Serves 2

½ CUP MAYONNAISE

½ CUP STORE-BOUGHT BOURBON MOLASSES OR STONE GROUND MUSTARD

1 TEASPOON FRESHLY SQUEEZED LEMON JUICE

4 SLICES TEXAS TOAST, TOASTED

2 SLICES GOUDA OR CHEDDAR CHEESE

HEIRLOOM TOMATOES, SLICED ½ INCH THICK

6–8 SLICES THICK-CUT HICKORY OR MAPLE BACON

½ CUP FRESH SPINACH

KOSHER SALT AND FRESHLY GROUND BLACK PEPPER

COLESLAW, FOR SERVING (OPTIONAL)

CUCUMBER SLICES, FOR SERVING (OPTIONAL)

In a medium bowl, mix together mayo, mustard, and lemon juice. Spread evenly over each piece of toast. On top of the toast, layer cheese, tomato, bacon, and spinach greens. Season with salt and pepper to taste. Serve with homemade coleslaw and freshly sliced cucumber.

CARAMEL AND DARK CHOCOLATE APPLES

These apples are a tradition in our household around the holidays. I make them every year as a little homemade treat for friends and family. Roll the chocolate-dipped apples in a wide variety of toppings, such as toasted coconut, crushed toffee pieces, crushed peppermint candies, hard-shell chocolate candies, or pretty much anything you can think of. These amazing treats are sure to be a huge hit!

Makes 12 apples

FOR THE CARAMEL:

2 CUPS FIRMLY PACKED BROWN SUGAR

1 CUP LIGHT CORN SYRUP

1/2 CUP (1 STICK) UNSALTED BUTTER

1/2 TEASPOON KOSHER SALT

1 (14-OUNCE) CAN SWEETENED CONDENSED MILK

1 TEASPOON PURE VANILLA EXTRACT

FOR THE APPLES:

12 GRANNY SMITH APPLES

12 (7-INCH) WOODEN STICKS

3–4 (4.4-OUNCE) DARK CHOCOLATE BARS, FINELY CHOPPED

12 CELLOPHANE BAGS

RIBBON OR NATURAL TWINE

MAKE THE CARAMEL:

In a large saucepan over medium heat, melt the sugar, corn syrup, butter, and salt. Stir occasionally with a wooden spoon to be sure the mixture does not burn. Once the mixture comes to a full boil, stir in the condensed milk. Continue to cook, stirring continuously with a wooden spoon, until a candy thermometer reaches 245 degrees F. Remove the pot from the heat and stir in the vanilla.

MAKE THE APPLES:

Line 2 baking sheets with parchment paper and set aside.

Twist the stems off of the apples. Push the wooden sticks into the center of the apples. (I use a small dish towel to protect hands from becoming bruised.) When the caramel has cooled, dip the apples into it. Gently shake off the excess caramel, set the apples onto the prepared baking sheets, and allow the caramel to harden.

Place the chocolate in a glass bowl, and then place the bowl over a small pot of simmering water. Be extremely careful not get any water or steam into the chocolate, or it will seize. Stir occasionally as the chocolate melts. Once the chocolate is partially melted, turn the heat off. Allow to sit for about 3 minutes, and stir any remaining lumps of chocolate until it is smooth.

Dip the caramel-covered apples into the chocolate. Shake off most of the excess chocolate, and then roll in any topping you desire. Place the apples immediately back on the parchment-lined baking pans to dry. Place the pans in a cool place until ready to package the apples. Package the apples individually in cellophane bags tied with ribbon.

MERRY YULE

NEW ENGLAND'S FINEST
CHRISTMAS TREE FARMS

There are many wonderful Christmas tree farms throughout New England. There is simply nothing like going out to the farm with your family and cutting down a fresh tree for the holidays, bringing home that comforting aroma of pine. In our family, it is a tradition that dates back to my childhood, and I do it now with my own children. We set aside the entire day to enjoy each other's company, beginning with breakfast and then heading out to harvest the perfect Christmas tree for our living room. Bringing Mother Nature inside our home always warms the spirit in our hearts.

The difference between cutting your own and getting a pre-cut tree is undeniable. Pre-cut trees are generally harvested in October in Vermont or Canada and shipped to area garden centers or nurseries. The problem is that they were harvested so long ago that many times they are just not fresh. Personally, my favorite varieties of Christmas trees include Balsam fir, white and blue spruce, and Fraser fir. Look for a tree that has a vibrant green color (or grayish-blue for blue spruce), is not losing pine needles, and has a straight trunk for easier placing in a tree stand. Cut the tree as close to the ground as you can, so not to leave much of a stump behind. Trees soak up a ton of water in the first three to four days, so it's imperative to water the tree twice a day for those first few days. If your tree stand dries up, the tree will form a seal and not be able to absorb any more water. The fresher you keep the tree, the nicer it will appear, along with being less of a fire hazard.

When decorating our tree, I put the lights on first, starting from the bottom and working my way up. We prefer the old-fashioned C7 lights because they produce more heat and make my vintage spinner ornaments twirl magically. They can be found on eBay, and while you're at it, be sure to check Etsy for great handmade ornaments and vintage finds, such as a Lifesaver garland like the one my grandmother bought me as a young child. When you attach lights to the tree, I find it gives more depth to weave the light strands in and out. That means you put a light on a branch inside the tree and work outwards, then repeat. This same technique applies with ornaments. I hang heavier ornaments inside the tree, where the branches tend to be thicker and are able to withstand more weight.

For natural decorations, pick up loose evergreens while you're at the tree farm and use them to fill flower pots on the porch. In December, a lush arrangement of evergreens adorn our fireplace mantle in a large Oasis floral piece. (Ask your local florist if you can purchase a casket saddle with Oasis floral foam.) Then, I decorate with an abundance of wonderful pinecones on picks, adding lush red roses the week of Christmas. Water the arrangement once daily to keep it as fresh as possible.

✦ **JONES FAMILY FARMS** in Shelton, Connecticut, is a seventh-generation 400-acre farm. They have been growing award-winning Christmas trees for over 60 years, with 200 acres of farmland completely devoted to fragrant evergreen trees. Spend the day hiking through the farm with the family and browse in their various barnyard shops, then taste their own farm-made wine in the winery's tasting room. The Harvest Kitchen serves up hot mulled cider, freshly baked cookies, and more, offering a full day's experience to absorb and enjoy.

✦ **MAPLE LANE FARM** in Preston, Connecticut, offers 35 acres of superb cut-your-own Christmas trees. In addition to a wide selection of different varieties of trees, this stunning farm also offers handmade wreaths, kissing balls, and garland. Join them on the weekends for a cup of hot chocolate while you browse the fields of pristine trees.

✦ **MAPLE ROW TREE FARM**, situated in Brookfield, Connecticut, has been growing some of the finest Christmas trees since the 1950s. On December weekends, they'll transport you on an old-fashioned tractor-drawn hayride to the area where you'll select the perfect tree. Their farm is 200 acres of pristine countryside with one of the largest selections of trees.

✦ **SLEIGHBELL TREE FARM** located in Sutton, Massachusetts, is a family-owned 10-acre Christmas tree farm. The O'Conner family grows Fraser and concolor firs, blue spruce, Scotch pine, and white pine. Stroll through their gift barn, full of handcrafted ornaments and locally made products. Sip hot cocoa and enjoy a hayride to the fields to select the perfect tree.

✦ **WERNER TREE FARM** in Middlebury, Vermont, offers the perfect way to kick off the holiday season by walking through the snow to select one of five varieties of fir trees. They also offer a limited amount of spruce for those who prefer that variety. This well-manicured farm also sells their own farm-made maple syrup, honey, maple cream, and candies. Their hand-woven wreaths and kissing balls will look great on your front door.

✦ **MEADOW RIDGE FARM** in Middlesex, Vermont, is currently maintaining more than 7,000 Christmas trees on their 8-acre farm. In 2001, Patrick and Tamara White bought the farm, which dates back to 1801 and has seen a wide variety of agriculture over the years. This meticulously maintained farm offers several varieties of perfectly trimmed trees to choose from. Visit their farm to cut your own fresh tree on Saturdays and Sundays starting Thanksgiving weekend right up until Christmas.

✦ **THE BISHOP FARM** in Springfield, Vermont, is now in its fifth generation of farming, with over 100 years of operating a tree farm. The farm specializes in growing Balsam and Fraser firs. On the weekend, take a ride on a wooden wagon, pulled by a tractor, to select your family's tree. Freshly made hot chocolate will keep you warm as you browse their handmade wreaths.

✦ **BAKERSFIELD TREE FARM** in Bakersfield, Vermont, started growing trees over 23 years ago, beginning with 5,000 trees and growing to 20,000. Their farm offers Colorado blue spruce, white pine, and Fraser, balsam, and Canaan firs. From Thanksgiving to December 24, walk the hills of their farm to choose your own Christmas tree. Owners Gary and Alice Foote are always at the farm to assist in any way.

✦ **THE RUSSELL FARM** in Starksboro, Vermont, is where owners David and Jane Russell offer old-fashioned horse-drawn sleigh rides to harvest trees. On the weekends from Thanksgiving to Christmas, pick out a handmade wreath with locally grown holly, or some Vermont-made maple syrup. Pack a picnic lunch and enjoy it by the pond or warm up in the cabin near the roaring wood fire.

✦ **THE OLD FARM CHRISTMAS PLACE** in Cape Elizabeth, Maine, is a family tradition in New England. Take a relaxing wagon ride to the top of the field to choose the perfect tree. The farm staff is ready to help load a fresh balsam fir tree or to drop it off at your home for convenience. Sip hot mulled cider and rich hot chocolate while browsing through the handmade ornaments in their charming post-and-beam store.

✦ **TUCKAWAY TREE FARM** in Lebanon, Maine, is owned and operated by Lynne Park and Susan Adams. They specialize in growing Balsam firs in a 7-acre field on their 27-acre farm. These very creative ladies also offer their own handmade wooden products such as bowls, plates, wine stoppers, and more. Create warm family memories with hot apple cider and tasty treats by the wood stove in their beautiful farm store, filled with handmade ornaments. Be sure to select a beautiful hand-crafted wreath to welcome guests into your home.

✦ **CLARKS CHRISTMAS TREE FARM**, established in 1958, is situated in historic Tiverton, Rhode Island, and grows Fraser, Douglas, and Canaan firs and spruce trees. Visit their gift store in a stunning post-and-beam barn for hot apple cider, handmade gifts, farm-fresh eggs, jams, maple syrup, artisan goat soap, and maple syrup. Walk through acres of gorgeously manicured trees and select the perfect one for your home.

✦ **BIG JOHN LEYDEN'S TREE FARM** in West Greenwich, Rhode Island, is well known for some of the area's prettiest trees. The farm grows over 100,000 trees in 10 different varieties. These gorgeously manicured Balsam, Fraser, and Douglas firs or blue spruces will leave your home full of evergreen fragrance for the entire holiday season. Let your kids climb on their vintage fire truck and ring the bell. Visiting this large farm will be an experience you'll want to continue on a yearly basis.

Be sure to carefully inspect the trunk of the tree to make sure it is straight. Selecting a crooked trunk could result in great difficulty getting it to stand straight in the stand.

Evergreen tree varieties that grow well in New England include:

- Colorado blue spruce (also known as blue spruce) has very sharp needles that are bluish-gray in color. These trees have a beautiful natural shape that needs very little pruning. They are becoming a popular choice for Christmas trees due to their symmetrical form, attractive blue foliage, and excellent needle retention. This variety also has very strong branches, which are helpful when hanging heavy ornaments.

- White spruce has a cone-shaped crown, blunt needles, and a bluish-green color. It's a wonderful variety for a Christmas tree because of its excellent foliage, good needle retention, great coloring, and wonderful natural shape.

- Norway spruce has a rich green color and incredible smell. The needle retention is considered poor unless the trees are freshly cut and kept watered properly.

- Balsam fir is one of the most popular choices in New England for a Christmas tree due to its pleasing aroma. It also has a wonderful dark-green appearance, long-lasting needles, and attractive form.

- Douglas fir offers a great aroma, has wonderful needle retention, and is soft to the touch. It has light-green coloring with medium-strong branches. This variety has very good needle retention and is one of my personal favorites.

- Fraser fir has flat needles that are dark green in color. Uniformly pyramid in shape, it features strong branches that turn slightly upward. This variety of Christmas tree is one of the best for needle retention, has a wonderful fragrance, and offers very soft needles.

- Canaan fir is similar to Fraser fir with its rich green color. It has soft, short needles and medium-strong branches. This particular tree has very good needle retention.

- Concolor fir has a thick and long needle that is bluish-gray in color. It has wonderful foliage, a beautiful natural shape, and retains its needles well.

BACON-WRAPPED MEATLOAF

New England winters can be pretty cold. Juicy meatloaf offers a wonderful, simple dinner and is best-served alongside creamy mashed potatoes. Use the leftovers for meatloaf sandwiches.

Serves 4 to 6

1 POUND (80-PERCENT LEAN) GROUND CHUCK

1 POUND GROUND PORK

¼ CUP HONEY BARBEQUE SAUCE, PLUS ADDITIONAL FOR MEATLOAF GLAZE

¼ CUP KETCHUP

3 LARGE EGGS, LIGHTLY BEATEN

1 CUP SEASONED BREAD CRUMBS

1 CUP GRATED FRESH PARMESAN CHEESE

½ CUP WHOLE MILK

3 TEASPOONS DRY MUSTARD

2 TEASPOONS ONION POWDER

1 TEASPOON GARLIC POWDER

KOSHER SALT AND FRESHLY GROUND BLACK PEPPER

6 SLICES BACON

Preheat the oven to 400 degrees F.

In a large bowl, mix together all of the ingredients, except the bacon, with clean hands, until well combined. Line a baking sheet with aluminum foil. Form the mixture into a loaf and place onto the baking sheet.

Layer the uncooked bacon over the top of the meatloaf and brush the top with the additional honey barbeque sauce. Bake until fully cooked, 45 to 50 minutes. Allow to sit for about 5 minutes before serving.

MULLED APPLE CIDER

This is a favorite in our house for holiday gatherings or fall and winter dinners. Perfect on a cold New England day, I heat it on the stove and then transfer it to a stainless-steel pump pot to keep piping hot. The smell of sugar and spices will welcome guests as they enter your home.

Serves 4 to 6

1 QUART APPLE CIDER

1 TABLESPOON GROUND CINNAMON

1 TEASPOON GROUND NUTMEG

½ TEASPOON GROUND CLOVES

2 TABLESPOONS BROWN SUGAR

In a large pot, combine all of the ingredients. Heat over medium-high heat, stirring occasionally, and cook for 15 to 20 minutes while flavors meld. Serve.

SOUR CREAM MASHED POTATOES

Mashed potatoes add the feeling of grandma's kitchen to any dinner, and these fluffy mashed potatoes are a perfect addition to any meatloaf or pot roast. I leave the skins on for a heartier flavor and texture.

Serves 6 to 8

6–8 MEDIUM TO LARGE RUSSET POTATOES, WASHED AND UNPEELED

½ CUP (1 STICK) UNSALTED BUTTER, CUT INTO PIECES

½ CUP HEAVY CREAM

½ CUP SOUR CREAM

KOSHER SALT AND FRESHLY GROUND BLACK PEPPER

Place the potatoes into a large pot and cover with cold water. Bring to a boil over high heat and cook the potatoes until they are tender. Drain the potatoes in a colander and return to the pot. Add the butter, heavy cream, and sour cream, and smash the mixture with a potato masher. Stir in the salt and pepper to taste. Cover the pot to keep the mashed potatoes warm until ready to serve.

TWICE-BAKED POTATOES

What's not to love about creamy mashed potatoes combined with shredded cheddar cheese and crisp bacon? Better still, these are super-simple to make. I usually make a few extra to freeze for later use.

Serves 8 to 10

10 LARGE RUSSET POTATOES

½ CUP (1 STICK) UNSALTED BUTTER, SOFTENED

1 CUP HEAVY CREAM

1 CUP SOUR CREAM

KOSHER SALT AND FRESHLY GROUND BLACK PEPPER

½ CUP COOKED CHOPPED BACON

1 CUP SHREDDED CHEDDAR CHEESE

SWEET PAPRIKA

Preheat the oven to 450 degrees F.

Line a sheet pan with parchment paper. Wash the potatoes and place them on the pan. Bake the potatoes until soft, about 1½ hours. Remove from the oven and allow to cool for 5 to 10 minutes. Do not turn off the oven.

Cut the potatoes in half lengthwise. Using a teaspoon, scoop out most of the potato into a mixing bowl, leaving a small amount behind to support the skin. Place the hollowed potato skins onto a baking sheet. Combine the potato flesh with butter, heavy cream, and sour cream; season with salt and pepper. Mix until thoroughly combined. With a spatula, fold in the bacon and cheddar cheese. Transfer the mashed potato mixture to a large ziplock bag. Cut off a corner of the ziplock bag and squeeze the mixture into the potato skins. Sprinkle the top of the potatoes with a light dusting of paprika. Bake for 30 to 35 minutes, until lightly golden brown.

FARMHOUSE OATMEAL– CHOCOLATE CHIP COOKIES

I'm pretty sure this will be your new favorite oatmeal–chocolate chip cookie. It's a recipe I developed a while back that yields the perfect combination of melted chocolate, oatmeal, and just a touch of maple sugar. For summer, make these cookies into ice cream sandwiches with your favorite flavor of ice cream. Place them in ziplock bags and keep in the freezer for a refreshing treat.

Makes about 3 dozen

1 CUP (2 STICKS) UNSALTED BUTTER, SOFTENED

½ CUP GRANULATED MAPLE SUGAR

1 CUP FIRMLY PACKED BROWN SUGAR

1 LARGE EGG

1 TEASPOON PURE VANILLA EXTRACT

1¾ CUPS ALL-PURPOSE FLOUR

1¼ CUPS OLD-FASHIONED ROLLED OATS

½ TEASPOON BAKING POWDER

½ TEASPOON BAKING SODA

1 TEASPOON KOSHER SALT

1½ CUPS SEMISWEET CHOCOLATE CHIPS

Preheat the oven to 375 degrees F. Line a baking sheet with parchment paper and set aside.

In a large bowl, use a hand mixer to cream together the butter, maple sugar, and brown sugar. Add the egg and vanilla and combine.

In another bowl, mix together the flour, oats, baking powder, baking soda, and salt. Gradually combine the dry ingredients with the creamed butter mixture. Stir the chocolate chips into the batter. Scoop out teaspoon-size balls onto the baking sheet. Bake for 9 to 11 minutes, until lightly golden brown. Allow to cool on a baking rack and enjoy.

CHOCOLATE-DRIZZLED CARAMEL POPCORN

This yummy treat will bring you back to your childhood. Add a few mixed nuts to turn this into a salty and sweet treat.

Serves 4 to 6

10–12 CUPS POPPED POPCORN

1 CUP (2 STICKS) UNSALTED BUTTER

2 CUPS FIRMLY PACKED BROWN SUGAR

½ CUP GRANULATED SUGAR

½ TEASPOON KOSHER SALT

½ CUP LIGHT CORN SYRUP

1 (14-OUNCE) CAN SWEETENED CONDENSED MILK

1 TEASPOON PURE VANILLA EXTRACT

½ TEASPOON BAKING SODA

2 CUPS SEMISWEET CHOCOLATE CHIPS

Preheat the oven to 250 degrees F.

Grease 2 baking sheets. Pour the freshly popped popcorn onto the baking sheets and put in the oven to keep warm. In a medium saucepan over low to medium heat, melt butter, brown sugar, granulated sugar, salt, and corn syrup. Once the sugars are melted, add the condensed milk, stirring occasionally with a wooden spoon until the mixture reaches 238 degrees F on a candy thermometer. Remove the caramel mixture from heat. Stir in the vanilla and baking soda.

Remove the popcorn from the oven, but do not turn off the heat. Pour the caramel over the popcorn and stir to coat evenly. Return the popcorn to the oven and bake until the caramel is bubbling and dark brown, about 25 minutes. Remove the popcorn from the oven and transfer to cooling racks. Meanwhile, set up a double boiler on the stovetop and melt the chocolate. Drizzle the chocolate over the popcorn and allow the chocolate to harden, 1 to 2 hours. Break apart caramel popcorn with your hands. Store in an airtight container in a cool, dry place.

OLD-FASHIONED GLAZED DOUGHNUTS

When I was little, my mom often made homemade doughnuts on her kitchen stove. I remember our golden retriever would sit, practically under her feet, patiently waiting for the doughnut holes to drop. Homemade doughnuts are relatively simple to make and oh-so-good!

Makes 18 doughnuts

FOR THE DOUGHNUTS:

2¼ TEASPOONS DRY ACTIVE YEAST

½ CUP WATER, LUKEWARM (115 DEGREES F)

½ CUP WHOLE MILK

⅓ CUP VEGETABLE SHORTENING, PLUS ADDITIONAL FOR FRYING

⅓ CUP SUGAR

½ TEASPOON KOSHER SALT

2 LARGE EGGS

3½–4 CUPS ALL-PURPOSE FLOUR

FOR THE GLAZE:

1 CUP POWDERED SUGAR

½ TEASPOON PURE VANILLA EXTRACT

1 TABLESPOON WHOLE MILK

In a small measuring cup, combine the yeast and lukewarm water. Stir and allow yeast to soften. In a medium saucepan over medium heat, bring the milk almost to a boil. Quickly stir in the shortening, sugar, and salt. Remove the mixture from heat and cool to lukewarm. Whisk in the reserved yeast mixture and eggs. Transfer the mixture into a large mixing bowl.

Stir the flour into the yeast mixture, adding enough flour to create a soft dough. When the dough pulls away from the sides of the bowl, transfer it onto a lightly floured surface. Knead until the dough becomes smooth. Add the dough to a greased bowl, cover with plastic wrap, and refrigerate overnight.

Line a baking sheet with parchment paper and set aside. Turn the dough out onto a lightly floured surface, and use a rolling pin to it roll out to ½ inch thickness. Lightly flour a doughnut cutter and use it to cut out the dough. Place the doughnut cutouts onto the prepared baking sheet, cover loosely with plastic wrap, and let rise in a warm place until doubled in size, about 1 hour.

In a medium heavy-duty pot, melt shortening to about 3 to 4 inches and heat it to 375 degrees F. Place only a few doughnuts in the oil to cook at a time, frying each doughnut for 2 to 3 minutes on each side, or until lightly golden brown. Drain on paper towels. In a small bowl, combine all of the glaze ingredients together. Drizzle the glaze over warm doughnuts.

APPLE CIDER DOUGHNUTS

Homemade doughnuts rolled in cinnamon sugar will remind you of days spent at an old-fashioned fair or the local apple orchard. The wonderful addition of small pieces of apples will make your mouth water.

Makes 18 doughnuts

1 CUP APPLE CIDER

4½ CUPS ALL-PURPOSE FLOUR

1 TABLESPOON BAKING POWDER

1 TEASPOON BAKING SODA

1 TEASPOON KOSHER SALT

2 TEASPOONS GROUND CINNAMON

½ TEASPOON GROUND NUTMEG

6 TABLESPOONS UNSALTED BUTTER, SOFTENED

½ CUP GRANULATED SUGAR

½ CUP FIRMLY PACKED BROWN SUGAR

2 LARGE EGGS, ROOM TEMPERATURE

½ CUP BUTTERMILK

1 TEASPOON PURE VANILLA EXTRACT

2 MEDIUM TO LARGE APPLES, PEELED, CORED, AND FINELY CHOPPED

VEGETABLE SHORTENING FOR FRYING

CINNAMON SUGAR:

1½ CUPS GRANULATED SUGAR

3 TABLESPOONS GROUND CINNAMON

1 TEASPOON NUTMEG

In a medium saucepan over low heat, reduce the apple cider to about ¾ cup, about 20 minutes. Set aside and cool to room temperature.

Sift together the flour, baking powder, baking soda, salt, and spices into a medium bowl and set aside. In a large bowl, use a hand mixer to cream together the butter granulated sugar, and brown sugar. Add the eggs one at a time and continue to mix until incorporated. Use a rubber spatula to occasionally scrape the sides and bottom of the bowl. Add the reserved reduced apple cider, buttermilk, and vanilla extract, mixing to combine. Add the flour mixture and combine. Gently fold the chopped apples into the batter.

Line a baking sheet with parchment paper and set aside. Turn the dough out onto a lightly floured surface, and use a rolling pin to roll out the dough to ½ inch thickness. Lightly flour a doughnut cutter and use it to cut out the doughnuts, then place them onto the prepared baking sheet.

Line a baking sheet with several layers of paper towels and set aside. In a large heavy-duty pot, add enough shortening to equal 3 inches of oil. Heat to a temperature of 375 degrees F. Drop about 4 doughnuts into the oil, making sure not to overcrowd the pot. Cook for 1 to 2 minutes on each side, or until lightly golden brown. Remove the doughnuts from the oil and allow to drain on the paper towels. In a small bowl, combine all of the ingredients for the cinnamon sugar; mix well. While the doughnuts are still warm, sprinkle them with the cinnamon sugar.

OLD-FASHIONED PUMPKIN DOUGHNUTS

When I was little, our golden retriever would sit near the stove, practically under my mother's feet, as she fried old-fashioned doughnuts. The dog knew my mother would occasionally "drop" a few doughnut holes. I put a new spin on my mother's recipe and developed something perfect for the cool fall weather. I think you'll love my old-fashioned pumpkin doughnuts. Next time you are in the grocery store, pick up a few cans of canned pumpkin puree and discover how simple these are to make.

Makes 18 doughnuts

6 TABLESPOONS UNSALTED BUTTER, SOFTENED

½ CUP SUGAR

½ CUP FIRMLY PACKED BROWN SUGAR

2 LARGE EGGS, ROOM TEMPERATURE

1 TEASPOON PURE VANILLA EXTRACT

4½ CUPS ALL-PURPOSE FLOUR

1 TABLESPOON BAKING POWDER

1 TEASPOON BAKING SODA

1 TEASPOON KOSHER SALT

1 CUP PUREED PUMPKIN

2 TEASPOONS GROUND CINNAMON

½ TEASPOON GROUND NUTMEG

½ CUP BUTTERMILK

CINNAMON SUGAR (PAGE 171)

1 TEASPOON GROUND NUTMEG

In a large mixing bowl, cream together the butter, sugar, and brown sugar. Add the eggs one at a time and the vanilla.

Sift the flour, baking powder, soda, and salt into a medium bowl.

Add the pumpkin, cinnamon, and nutmeg to the sugar mixture. Alternate adding the buttermilk and dry ingredients until everything is combined. Use a rubber spatula to scrape the sides and bottom of the mixing bowl occasionally.

Turn the dough out onto a lightly floured work surface. Roll out to about ½ inch thick and use a doughnut cutter to cut out the doughnuts. Place the doughnuts and doughnut holes on sheet pans lined with parchment paper.

Line another sheet pan with several layers of paper towels and set aside.

In a large pot, heat about 3 inches of canola oil to 375 degrees F. Use a thermometer to test the temperature. Gently drop about 4 doughnuts into the hot oil, do not overcrowd the pot. Cook for about 1 to 2 minutes on each side, flipping the doughnut once. Remove doughnuts from the oil and let drain on paper towels. Coat with Cinnamon Sugar while still warm.

MADE IN
NEW ENGLAND
WITH LOVE
OLD-FASHIONED
COUNTRY STORES

In every corner of New England, there are amazing old-fashioned country stores. Many have been around for hundreds of years and are still bursting at the seams with quality products. These country stores, or general stores, were originally founded out of necessity for pioneers. In the 19th century, daily life revolved around going to the local general store to pick up a yard of fabric and denim overalls, as well as root beer barrel candies for well-behaved kids and feed for animals on the homestead. Not only did these stores sell hardware, sewing supplies, produce, household items, and farm supplies, they were often a post office and local community center as well. When you visit these stores today, it is as if you are stepping back in time. Walk through an old screen door that slams shut behind you and step onto the rickety wide-plank wooden floor. All of these stores offer a wide array of New England cheeses, candy, specialty foods, and handcrafted items. Many of them also offer hard-to-find specialty foods, beautiful hand-sewn quilts, wooden toys, and freshly baked New England treats. These old-fashioned country stores bring back so many memories, and they are a wonderful place to create new ones.

✦ WILLIAMSBURG GENERAL STORE, in Williamsburg, Massachusetts, has its own bakery, where you can purchase homemade breads, pastries, and cookies, all made from scratch daily. The old-fashioned store has beautiful hardwood floors, shelves full of locally made Hogwash (old-fashioned glycerin soap), bulk spices, unique handmade gifts, and much more. Before you leave, grab a creamy ice cream cone with two scoops of your favorite flavor.

✦ WAYSIDE COUNTRY STORE is situated in Marlborough, Massachusetts. Built in 1790, it originally stood in the center of Sudbury, Massachusetts. Henry Ford purchased the building in 1928 and moved it by oxen to its current location. Shelves filled with wooden toys will transport you back in time, but make sure you also browse their beautiful pottery and locally made jams and preserves.

✦ HOPE GENERAL STORE sits on the mid-coast of Hope, Maine. Operating as a general store since 1832, they continue to provide New England–crafted products to their customers. This colonial clapboard–style store is rustic and so very charming. Tempt your taste buds with one of their signature sandwiches at the deli and grab a bottle of locally made soda pop.

✦ THE NEWFANE COUNTRY STORE in Newfane, Vermont, offers the charm of New England with a front porch, original wood floors, and old-fashioned penny candy. There are also gorgeous handmade quilts by local Vermont quilters; pick out a stunning quilt from the selection in the store or have one custom made. They have a wide assortment of locally produced gourmet food, maple syrup, honey, and handmade pottery. You'll also find wooden trains that are made in Vermont and handmade cutting boards.

✦ THE ORIGINAL GENERAL STORE in Pittsfield, Vermont, offers a full-service deli to enjoy a true Vermont breakfast or a tasty lunch. Find beautiful handmade pottery, locally roasted coffee, maple syrup, hand-carved furniture, and an assortment of New England products.

✦ ZEB'S GENERAL STORE sits in the picturesque town of North Conway, New Hampshire. This beautiful, nostalgic general store features natural wood floors and wall-to-ceiling wooden shelves filled with New England–made specialty products. Farmhouse-style galvanized tables display an enormous array of vintage candies, kitchen accessories, and books.

PÂTÉ CHINOIS

Pâté Chinois is the French-Canadian version of shepherd's pie, made with ground beef on the bottom, a layer of creamed corn, and topped with creamy mashed potatoes. Baking it in the oven gives the potatoes a crispy crust. This dish is often served during the colder months of the year and has been a winter staple on our dinner table for as long as I can remember. Serve with a warm piece of bread dripping with melted butter and, of course, plenty of ketchup! For a variation, sprinkle 1 cup shredded cheddar on top of the potatoes before baking.

Serves 4 to 6

4–5 BACON SLICES, CHOPPED

1 LARGE ONION, CHOPPED

1 POUND (80% LEAN) GROUND CHUCK

6–8 MEDIUM TO LARGE RUSSET POTATOES, PEELED AND CHOPPED

½ CUP (1 STICK) UNSALTED BUTTER, SOFTENED

½ CUP HEAVY CREAM

½ CUP SOUR CREAM

KOSHER SALT AND FRESHLY GROUND BLACK PEPPER

1 (15-OUNCE) CAN CREAMED CORN

SWEET PAPRIKA

Preheat the oven to 375 degrees F.

In a large pan over medium heat, sauté the bacon and onion. Cook for about 10 minutes, occasionally stirring with a wooden spoon. Add the ground chuck to the pan and sauté until fully cooked. Transfer the beef mixture to a 3-quart glass baking dish, spreading it in an even layer. Add the potatoes to a large pot, cover with cold water, and sprinkle with a little salt. Cook over high heat until tender.

Drain the potatoes into a colander, and then transfer them back into the pot. Add the butter, heavy cream, and sour cream; season with salt and pepper. Using a hand mixer, beat the potatoes until creamy.

Pour the creamed corn evenly over the ground beef in the dish. Then spread the potatoes evenly over the corn. Sprinkle lightly with paprika. Bake until golden brown, about 35 minutes.

FARMHOUSE MILK & HONEY DINNER ROLLS

Homemade rolls take a little bit of time to make but are so worth the effort. You'll never want to buy store-bought again. These delicious rolls make great sandwiches too.

Makes 12 to 18 rolls

1 1/2 TEASPOONS ACTIVE DRY YEAST

1 1/4 CUPS WHOLE MILK, WARM (115 DEGREES F)

1/4 CUP HONEY

1/4 CUP (1/2 STICK) UNSALTED BUTTER, MELTED

1 TEASPOON KOSHER SALT

4 1/2–5 CUPS ALL-PURPOSE FLOUR

In a large mixing bowl, dissolve the yeast in the warm milk. Add the honey, butter, salt, and 2 cups flour. Using a hand mixer, beat until smooth. Add enough of the remaining flour to form a soft dough. Turn the dough onto a lightly floured surface and knead until smooth and elastic, 6 to 8 minutes. Grease a large bowl and place the dough in the bowl, turning once to grease the top. Cover the dough loosely with plastic wrap and let rise in a warm place until doubled, about 1 hour. Line a baking sheet with parchment paper.

Punch down the dough and shape into 12 to 18 small dinner rolls. Transfer the rolls to the prepared baking sheet, leaving enough space for the rolls to rise. Cover loosely with plastic wrap and let rise until doubled, about 35 to 40 minutes. Preheat the oven to 350 degrees F. When the rolls have risen, bake for 25 to 30 minutes, or until golden brown. Serve the rolls warm with farm-fresh butter.

CHOCOLATE CREAM PIE

If I have learned anything about French-Canadian men, it's that you always serve bread with dinner, and dessert is a must. This chocolate-custard pie is a delicious treat to solve any sweet cravings.

Serves 4 to 6

FOR THE CRUST:

1 1/2 CUPS ALL-PURPOSE FLOUR

1/2 TEASPOON KOSHER SALT

1/4 CUP VEGETABLE SHORTENING, CHILLED

1/4 CUP (1/2 STICK) UNSALTED BUTTER, CHILLED AND CUT INTO PIECES

3–4 TABLESPOONS ICE-COLD WATER

FOR THE CHOCOLATE CUSTARD:

5 LARGE EGG YOLKS

1 1/2 CUPS GRANULATED SUGAR

1/3 CUP CORNSTARCH

1/2 TEASPOON KOSHER SALT

2 CUPS WHOLE MILK

1 CUP HEAVY CREAM

3 OUNCES UNSWEETENED BAKING CHOCOLATE

FOR THE WHIPPED TOPPING:

1 CUP HEAVY CREAM

1/4 CUP GRANULATED SUGAR

Preheat the oven to 375 degrees F. In a large bowl, combine the flour and salt. Use a fork to cut the shortening and butter into the flour until the mixture resembles coarse meal. Add 3 tablespoons of the water. Turn the dough onto a lightly floured surface and gently form the dough into a ball with your hands, adding more water if needed. Using a rolling pin, roll the dough out to about 1/2 inch thickness. Transfer the dough to a 9-inch pie plate and press it into the bottom and around the side. Roll the edges under and press the crust between your fingers. Fill the unbaked pie shell with pie weights and bake until lightly golden, 30 to 35 minutes.

To make the custard, in a small bowl add the egg yolks and beat with a fork. In a medium saucepan over low to medium heat, combine the sugar, cornstarch, and salt. Gradually add the milk, heavy cream, and chocolate, stirring continuously with a wooden spoon. Continue to cook until the mixture starts to boil and thicken. Boil for 1 minute, continuing to stir. Stir half of the hot mixture into the egg yolks, then pour the hot egg mixture back into the saucepan. Boil for 1 minute. Remove from heat and pour into the prepared pie crust. To prevent a tough layer from forming on the custard, cover with plastic wrap, pressing directly onto the chocolate custard. Refrigerate for 3 to 4 hours.

To make the topping, in a large bowl add the heavy cream and the sugar. Using a hand mixer, whip until firm peaks form. Remove the plastic wrap from the chilled pie, and spread the whipped cream over the top. Stick toothpicks into the pie and cover loosely with plastic wrap. Keep refrigerated until ready to serve.

FARMHOUSE BUTTERMILK BISCUITS

These biscuits are full of melt-in-your-mouth goodness. Beautiful layers of fluffy biscuits are perfect with melted butter or homemade berry jam, or for making tempting breakfast sandwiches.

Makes 6 to 9

2¾ CUPS ALL-PURPOSE FLOUR

1 TABLESPOON BAKING POWDER

½ TEASPOON BAKING SODA

1 TEASPOON KOSHER SALT

⅓ CUP LARD OR VEGETABLE SHORTENING

4 TABLESPOONS UNSALTED BUTTER, COLD

1 CUP BUTTERMILK

Preheat the oven to 400 degrees F. Line a baking sheet with parchment paper and set aside.

In a large bowl, combine the flour, baking powder, baking soda, and salt. Use a fork or pastry cutter to cut the shortening and butter into the flour until the mixture resembles coarse meal. Gradually stir in the buttermilk until the dough pulls away from the sides of the bowl.

Turn the dough out onto a lightly floured surface. Gently knead the dough 12 to 15 times. Using a rolling pin, roll out the dough to about ½ to ¾ inch thickness. Use a biscuit cutter 2½ to 3 inches in size to cut out the biscuits from the dough. Place them on the prepared baking sheet. Bake until lightly golden brown, 18 to 20 minutes.

SWEET SUMMER LOBSTER ROLLS

Lobster rolls are the street food of the rocky Maine coast. They pair perfectly with my Farmhouse Sweet & Tangy Pickles (page 134) and some kettle chips.

Makes 4 rolls

4 LOBSTERS (ABOUT 1¼ POUNDS EACH)

⅓ CUP MAYONNAISE

1 TEASPOON DIJON MUSTARD

2 TABLESPOONS FRESH SQUEEZED LEMON JUICE

2 TABLESPOONS FINELY CHOPPED CELERY

PINCH OF SMOKED PAPRIKA

KOSHER SALT AND FRESHLY GROUND BLACK PEPPER

4 SPLIT-TOP HOT DOG BUNS

2 TABLESPOONS MELTED BUTTER

4 PIECES BOSTON LETTUCE

Bring a large pot of salted water to a boil. Add the lobsters and cook until they turn bright red, about 10 minutes. While the lobsters are cooking, prepare an ice-water bath in a large bowl. Using tongs, plunge the hot lobsters into the ice-water bath for 5 to 6 minutes to cool; drain. Twist off the tails and claws, removing the meat from each. Remove and discard the intestinal vein that runs the length of each tail. Cut the meat into ½-inch pieces; rinse with water and drain in a strainer set over a bowl; discard the dirty water. Transfer the meat to a medium bowl and refrigerate until very cold, at least 1 hour.

In a large bowl, mix the chilled lobster with the mayonnaise, mustard, lemon juice, celery, and paprika; season with salt and pepper to taste.

Heat a large cast-iron skillet over medium heat. Brush the sides of the hot dog buns with melted butter. Toast the buns in the skillet until moderately golden brown on both sides. Place the toasted buns onto serving plates. Line each bun with a piece of lettuce and spoon the lobster salad over the top. Serve immediately.

CHEESECAKE BROWNIES

There is nothing better than mixing two of New England's most delicious desserts: rich, decadent chocolate brownies swirled with a cream cheese filling. You will be eating every little crumb left behind.

Makes 12

FOR THE BROWNIES:

¾ CUP (1½ STICKS) UNSALTED BUTTER

5 OUNCES UNSWEETENED BAKING CHOCOLATE

1¾ CUPS GRANULATED SUGAR

1 TEASPOON PURE VANILLA EXTRACT

4 LARGE EGGS

1½ CUPS ALL-PURPOSE FLOUR

½ TEASPOON KOSHER SALT

FOR THE CREAM CHEESE FILLING:

4 OUNCES CREAM CHEESE, SOFTENED

1 LARGE EGG

½ CUP GRANULATED SUGAR

1 TEASPOON PURE VANILLA EXTRACT

1 TEASPOON FRESH SQUEEZED LEMON JUICE

Preheat the oven to 325 degrees F. Grease an 8 x 8-inch glass baking dish and set aside.

In a medium saucepan over low to medium heat, melt the butter and chocolate, stirring occasionally. Remove the chocolate from the heat. In a large bowl, whisk together the sugar, vanilla and eggs. Add the melted chocolate mixture and combine. Add the flour and salt and mix well, using a spatula to scrape the sides of the bowl.

In a large bowl, add the all the ingredients for the cream cheese filling, mixing well to combine. Pour three-fourths of the brownie batter into the prepared baking dish. Spread the cream cheese filling over the brownie batter. Drop the remaining brownie batter over the cream cheese filling. Carefully spread the batter over the cream cheese, and then gently swirl the two together using a butter knife. Bake for 50 to 60 minutes, until a toothpick inserted in the center comes out clean.

FARMHOUSE APPLE CRISP

This is a recipe I developed for my parents' farm to sell at local farmers markets. The unique flavor comes from granulated maple sugar, which harbors a distinct sweet flavor. Granulated maple sugar, a New England tradition, can be substituted in many recipes to add that wonderful, rich sweet flavor. For this crisp, I use whatever tart apple is in season to give the perfect mix of tart and sweet.

Makes 6 to 8 servings

1 CUP (2 STICKS) UNSALTED BUTTER, SOFTENED

1 CUP FIRMLY PACKED BROWN SUGAR

¾ CUP GRANULATED MAPLE SUGAR

2 CUPS ALL-PURPOSE FLOUR

½ TEASPOON KOSHER SALT

1 CUP ROLLED OATS

1 TEASPOON GROUND CINNAMON

½ TEASPOON GROUND NUTMEG

7–8 LARGE APPLES

HOMEMADE VANILLA ICE CREAM, FOR SERVING

Preheat oven to 400 degrees F. Grease a 9 x 13-inch baking pan with vegetable shortening and set aside.

In a large mixing bowl, use a hand mixer to cream together the butter, brown sugar, and maple sugar. Add the flour, salt, oats, cinnamon, and nutmeg, thoroughly combining the mixture.

Peel, core, and slice the apples. Add the apple slices to the prepared pan. Cover apples with the oat mixture and spread it out evenly with your hands. Cover with aluminum foil and bake for about 30 minutes. Uncover and continue baking until lightly golden brown, about 20 more minutes. Serve warm with ice cream.

INDEX

METRIC CONVERSION CHART

VOLUME MEASUREMENTS		WEIGHT MEASUREMENTS		TEMPERATURE CONVERSION	
U.S.	Metric	U.S.	Metric	Fahrenheit	Celsius
1 teaspoon	5 ml	1/2 ounce	15 g	250	120
1 tablespoon	15 ml	1 ounce	30 g	300	150
1/4 cup	60 ml	3 ounces	90 g	325	160
1/3 cup	75 ml	4 ounces	115 g	350	180
1/2 cup	125 ml	8 ounces	225 g	375	190
2/3 cup	150 ml	12 ounces	350 g	400	200
3/4 cup	175 ml	1 pound	450 g	425	220
1 cup	250 ml	2 1/4 pounds	1 kg	450	230